Brookings Occasional Papers

Allied Rights and Legal Constraints on German Military Power

P A U L   B .   S T A R E S

Research Associate
Foreign Policy Studies Program

THE BROOKINGS INSTITUTION
Washington, D. C.

Brookings Occasional Papers

THE BROOKINGS INSTITUTION is a private nonprofit organization devoted to research, education, and publication on important issues of domestic and foreign policy. Its principal purpose is to bring knowledge to bear on the major policy problems facing the American people.

On occasion Brookings staff members produce research papers that warrant immediate circulation as contributions to the public debate on current issues of national importance. Because of the speed of their production, these Occasional Papers are not subjected to all of the formal review procedures established for the Institution's research publications, and they may be revised at a later date. As in all Brookings publications, the judgments, conclusions, and recommendations presented in the Papers are solely those of the authors and should not be ascribed to the trustees, officers, or other staff members of the Institution.

Allied Rights and Legal Constraints
on German Military Power

Contents

Acknowledgements

The author is grateful to many persons for their assistance in the preparation of this monograph. In particular, he would like to thank Alice Ackermann, Richard K. Betts, Ivo Daalder, Catherine M. Kelleher, John D. Steinbruner, and Steven Szabo for their valuable comments on early drafts of this study, as well as several U.S. government officials who wish to remain anonymous. Needless to say, they are absolved of any responsibility for its contents. The author is also grateful to Elisa Harris, Col. Eckart Fisher, Dagmar Kraemer, and Wolfgang Reinicke for help along the way. Finally, Drew Portocarrero provided admirable research support throughout the project, and Annette D. Proctor helped with the word processing. Preparation of the manuscript for publication was the work of Caroline Lalire, Ken Sabol, and Ann M. Ziegler.

Brookings gratefully acknowledges the financial support for this project provided by the John D. and Catherine T. MacArthur Foundation and the Carnegie Corporation of New York.

I: Introduction

Even after the breathtaking events of 1989 had seemingly made anything possible in Europe, few would have imagined that the two German states would become unified within a year. But that is precisely what will be concluded with the first all-German elections scheduled for December 2, 1990. As recently as July, however, this outcome was still in some doubt, principally because of Soviet opposition to the prospect of a united Germany becoming a member of the opposing North Atlantic Treaty Organization (NATO) and having no limits on the size of its armed forces. Since the Soviet Union could in principle withhold its consent to reunification as one of the vestigial rights it retained (along with its former allies Great Britain, France, and the United States) after the Second World War and also refuse to remove its large contingent of forces from East Germany, these concerns could not be dismissed lightly. As a result, however, of the agreement reached between West German Chancellor Helmut Kohl and Soviet President Mikhail Gorbachev at Zheleznovodsk in the USSR on July 16, 1990, the diplomatic logjam was broken and the way made clear for unification.

Under the terms of this agreement, the Soviet Union accepted Germany's sovereign right to membership in NATO and agreed to a phased withdrawal of its forces from German soil over a period of three to four years. In return, the German government pledged that it will reduce its armed forces to a level no higher than 370,000 personnel, to be implemented likewise over a three-to-four-year period as part of a Conventional Forces in Europe (CFE) agreement. It was also agreed that the territory of the former German Democratic Republic (GDR) would be covered by the security provisions of the North Atlantic Treaty from the date of unification, but that NATO forces—including nuclear weapon delivery systems—would be prohibited from entering this area while Soviet troops remained there. A united Germany, furthermore, would refrain from manufacturing nuclear, biological, and chemical weapons and remain a signatory of the Nuclear Non-Proliferation Treaty.[1]

With the earlier obstacles swept aside, the negotiations between the two German states and the four former allied powers—the so-called Two plus Four talks—which began in February 1990 to address the external aspects of German unification, are to be speedily concluded in a final settlement that confers full sovereignty on the new German state. In the process the rights and responsibili-

1

ties retained by the four powers with respect to Germany will be formally terminated. The nature and extent of these rights, however, are neither widely known nor well understood even now that they are about to be signed away. Many may consider them either moribund or no longer significant, but that is far from true. In essence, they boil down to the right to determine the status of Germany "as a whole" including its territorial boundaries, jointly administer Berlin, and station military forces on German soil. This bare description, however, does not convey the full extent of allied rights. Indeed their scope would astound most observers, and even many experts. The primary purpose of this brief study, therefore, is to shed light on what the four powers are about to relinquish with the unification of Germany.

This review, covered in section two, will also illuminate what is *not* likely to be resolved by the "Final Settlement" document on Germany. Many of the issues relating to allied rights were considered too complex or too sensitive to be discussed within the Two plus Four talks. As a result, they were deliberately excluded and left for other more appropriate diplomatic settings to address. As Michael Young, deputy legal adviser to the U.S. Department of State, stated in testimony before the Senate Foreign Relations Committee:

> We believe that the settlement document should be brief. It must make a few important but technical adjustments to make the legal situation in Germany correspond to the new political realities there. No more is needed. Moreover, the Final Settlement on Germany is not the appropriate document in which to address the many detailed technical policy issues between the various parties. These can and will be settled elsewhere, bilaterally and multilaterally, as sovereign acts of a united Germany.[2]

The most likely issues to be discussed in follow-on negotiations concern allied rights to engage in intelligence-gathering operations from German soil, allied protection of German airspace, basing privileges, and certain other special defense arrangements that are discussed in greater detail below. It is also just a matter of time before the presence of all foreign forces in Germany—not just the Soviets'—becomes a matter for review and public debate. Once Soviet forces leave East Germany and perceptions of a military threat decline still further, substantial domestic pressure could grow on both sides of the Atlantic to remove all foreign forces and all nuclear weapons from Germany.

It is also fair to assume that the question of Germany's future military status will grow in prominence once unification takes place. In particular, the legal constraints that the two German states accepted on their military power and freedom of action as part of the price for rearmament will surely become the focus of intense scrutiny and possible revision. Already the constitutional limitations on the use of military force, which indirectly affect where German armed forces can be legitimately deployed, have prompted a major debate within the Federal Republic about its possible participation in military operations in the Persian Gulf.[3] Other special limits likely to attract attention apply to the size and structure of German armed forces, their command and control arrangements, and the latitude to develop certain types of armaments, notably nuclear weapons. Like the allied rights, these legal constraints are also not widely known or understood even in Germany. To help rectify this deficiency, section three of this study will take stock of the relevant agreements that currently circumscribe German military power.

The Germans recognized these constraints as not only inevitable given their past history but also desirable to assuage their neighbors' concerns about German rearmament. By and large they have had their intended effect; fears of German nationalistic aspirations have subsided while military stability in Europe has been enhanced. The argument could grow in Germany, however, that after forty years of exemplary international behavior, these constraints are anachronistic, discriminatory, and no longer necessary. But to those who remain fearful about possible German military aggrandizement and aggression, the constraints are sure to be viewed as essential for the maintenance of stability. While Germany must remain sensitive to these concerns, the most fruitful way for allaying whatever latent fears exist about a united Germany's military potential, without "singularizing" it in a way that breeds the kind of pernicious resentment that grew up after the punitive Versailles Treaty, is to reach a set of common security arrangements and guarantees for the whole of Europe. With the end of the cold war, unprecedented opportunities exist to achieve this through a combination of CFE reductions, confidence and security building measures (CSBMs), and the permanent institutionalization of the Conference on Security and Cooperation in Europe (CSCE).

II: Allied Rights

The task of determining the nature of allied rights in Germany is not a straightforward one. No document exists that lays them out in a clear and comprehensive form.[4] Instead there are a multitude of agreements and legal instruments of varying kinds that collectively define the retained rights of the four powers. These can be grouped into several categories. There are first the original quadripartite agreements between the United States, the Soviet Union, Great

Britain, and France. As originally understood by the four powers, these were only to be temporarily held until the terms of unconditional surrender were fulfilled and a final peace settlement was reached with Germany. With the outbreak of the cold war—in no small part due to fundamental differences in policy toward Germany—a peace conference was never convened, leaving unresolved many outstanding questions from the war and leaving Germany in a state of legal limbo.[5] Although many of the rights enjoyed by the allies as occupying powers were formally relinquished with the creation of two "sovereign" German states—the Federal Republic of Germany (FRG) and the German Democratic Republic—the primary quadripartite rights remained in force. These have been reaffirmed in miscellaneous tripartite agreements between the three Western allies and the Federal Republic of Germany. The Soviet Union did much the same thing in bilateral arrangements with the GDR. In the process of handing over "sovereignty" to the two German states, however, other rights were retained that do not fall neatly within the category of quadripartite rights, even though they are sometimes mistakenly confused with them. Some, but not all, of these secondary allied rights have lapsed from neglect, while others have been superseded by domestic legislation as well as by international treaties to which the two Germanies freely acceded. These will also be discussed where relevant. While the intention here is to be as comprehensive as possible, some of the legally binding agreements remain classified and therefore beyond public review.

Rather than discuss each of the relevant agreements in turn, this section focuses on the principal areas in which the allies have enjoyed certain rights. These comprise the following:

> (i)   the status of Germany "as a whole";
> (ii) the territorial borders of Germany;
> (iii) allied administration and access to Berlin; and
> (iv) the stationing of foreign forces on German soil.

For reference purposes the most important documents have been reproduced either fully or partially in several appendixes at the end of the study.

The Status of Germany "as a Whole"

The retained rights of the four powers are often reduced to the shorthand formulation of "matters relating to Germany as a whole." Though never explicitly defined, this term is generally accepted to mean the right to determine the territorial boundaries and political status of a unified Germany at a final peace settlement. It was never very clear, especially after the four powers repeatedly stressed German rights of self-determination, whether the allied powers enjoyed the final say in such matters or merely the right to be heard.

To understand the meaning of these rights necessitates going back to the agreements reached among the allies in the latter stages of the Second World War and the period immediately following the capitulation of the Third Reich. On September 12, 1944, in London, the United States, the United Kingdom, and the Soviet Union signed the Protocol on Zones of Occupation in Germany and Administration of the "Greater Berlin" Area (see document A1).[6] This agreement divided the territory of Germany, as bounded by its frontiers on December 31, 1937, into three zones of occupation, with France gaining a separate zone at a later date.[7] Not long afterward on November 14, 1944, the three allied powers, under the auspices of the European Advisory Commission set up to prepare for the defeat of Germany, signed the Agreement on Control Machinery in Germany (see doc. A4).[8] This agreement conferred "supreme authority" to the commanders-in-chiefs of the three powers in their respective zones of occupation and "jointly, in matters affecting Germany as a whole." An Allied Control Council was also established to administer Germany during the immediate period of occupation and ensure that Germany complied with the basic requirements of unconditional surrender. The question of longer-term allied control and administration, however, was deferred to a later date.[9]

After the German forces had surrendered in 1945, the four victorious powers issued a joint Declaration Regarding the Defeat of Germany and the Assumption of Supreme Authority by the Allied Powers in Berlin on June 5, 1945 (see doc. A5).[10] In it they reaffirmed their "supreme authority with respect to Germany," while renouncing any intention to annex it, and furthermore stated their right to "determine . . . the status of Germany or of any area at present being part of German territory." These rights were later restated in the Protocol of the Proceedings of the Berlin (Potsdam) Conference, signed on August 1, 1945 (see doc. A6).[11]

Although the attempt to administer Germany jointly eventually failed, the three Western allies were careful to note that their rights and responsibilities with respect to Germany "as a whole" remained unchanged in several subsequent agreements, notably those merging their zones of occupation in 1949, bestowing limited sovereignty to the FRG in the same year, and terminating the occupation regime in 1954.[12] Similar pronouncements were made by the Soviet Union in various diplomatic notes to the Western allies and in their bilateral agreements with the GDR.[13]

The Territorial Boundaries of Germany

Under the Berlin Declaration on the defeat of Germany (doc. A3), the four powers assumed the right to "determine the boundaries of Germany or of any part thereof." Accordingly, at the Potsdam conference (doc. A4) the allies reached *preliminary* agreement that "pending the final determination of Poland's western frontier," the Oder-Neisse line would bound the Soviet zone of occupation with Poland.[14] While the four powers reached no subsequent determination on Germany's territorial boundaries, they have restated their rights to do so on several occasions.[15]

Following the amalgamation of the western zones of occupation and the creation of the FRG, Britain, France, and the United States also reserved certain rights with regard to the policing and protection of West German airspace. Under the Convention on the Settlement of Matters Arising Out of the War and Occupation, May 26, 1952, As Amended by Schedule IV of the Protocol on Termination of the Occupation Regime in Germany (doc. B4), which was signed at Paris on October 23, 1954, the three powers stated that they would "continue to exercise control with respect to aircraft of the Union of the Soviet Socialist Republics utilizing the air space of the Federal Republic." [16] Separate tripartite arrangements also evidently govern the defense of FRG airspace, though the details remain classified. It is understood, for example, that only British or U.S. aircraft have the authority to make the first contact with intruders of West German airspace.[17] Furthermore, the decision to use force in such circumstances apparently rests with either a British or U.S. air force officer.[18] Since the French have no aircraft based on German soil, they have relinquished their responsibilities in this regard to Britain and the United States. Given the level of control that the Soviet Union has traditionally maintained over the activities of the GDR's military forces, it would not be surprising to find similar agreements in effect for the protection of East German airspace.

Allied Administration and Access to Berlin

Allied rights with respect to Berlin can be grouped into two basic categories: administration of the city and rights of access to it. The former can be traced back to the 1944 London Protocol (doc. A1), which, in addition to dividing Germany into zones of occupation, created a special area known as "Greater Berlin" and split it into three sectors (with a fourth added later for the French) to be jointly administered by the allies. An Inter-Allied Governing Authority, or "Allied Kommandatura," was also created as the central body for administering Berlin.[19]

Following the cessation of hostilities and the allied occupation of Berlin, arrangements were also reached among the four powers guaranteeing air, road, rail, and water access to the city. On June 29, 1945, military representatives of the three allied powers agreed in the first instance to establish surface links between the western zones of occupation and Berlin.[20] The only road link for military traffic running from Checkpoint Alpha at Helmstedt to Checkpoint Bravo in West Berlin derives from this agreement, although three civilian access routes were later added. On November 30, 1945, the Allied Control Council formally approved the establishment of three air corridors between Berlin and the western zones of occupation: Decision of the Control Council Approving Establishment of Berlin–Hamburg, Berlin–Buckeburg (Hannover), and Berlin–Frankfurt-am-Main Air Corridors (doc. A8).[21] Air access by these routes was later reaffirmed in the Revised Regulations Governing Flights in Air Corridors in Germany and the Berlin Control Zone, issued by the Air Directorate on October 22, 1946 (doc. A9).[22] Only military aircraft and civilian carriers registered in the United States, the United Kingdom, and France were allowed to use them, however. Besides consolidating and expanding miscellaneous regulations for using the air corridors, this agreement also established the Berlin Air Safety Center (BASC), which remains today the only vestige of four-power administration in Berlin.

Allied rights of access to Berlin were put to a severe test in the first of a series of crises when the Soviets blockaded surface routes to the city in 1948. The subsequent Berlin airlift and Western protestations of their legal rights eventually forced the Soviets to back down. In a four-power communiqué issued on May 4, 1949, all restrictions on communications, transport, and trade with Berlin were lifted (see doc. A10).[23] During the course of the crisis, however, the Soviet Union walked out of the Allied Kommandatura on July 1, 1948, thus ending—with the exception of Spandau Prison and the Berlin Air Safety Center—joint four-power administration of Berlin.[24] The Western allies, nevertheless, have repeatedly maintained ever since that the Kommandatura remains the supreme authority for "Greater Berlin" and, moreover, that their rights and responsibilities remain in effect despite the Soviet decision to cease participation in the joint administration of the city. Accordingly, the Western powers have continued to convene the Allied Kommandatura and exercise their rights under its jurisdiction.

Thus, the Western powers approved the constitutions of the Federal Republic and Berlin in 1949 and 1950, respectively, but denied the city on each occasion the right to become a separate state (*Land*) of the FRG.[25] Berlin's special status was further underlined by the Western allies in their legally binding stipulations regarding Berlin's inclusion in international undertakings of the Federal Republic.[26] And following the creation of the GDR in 1949, they also refused to recognize Berlin as its capital; in the Western view East Berlin still constitutes the Soviet zone of "Greater Berlin." As a consequence, the U.S. embassy in East Berlin is accredited "to the GDR" and not "in the GDR." To exercise their freedom of movement in the city the Western allies continued to send small military contingents, commonly known as flag patrols, into East Berlin on a regular basis.[27]

The Western allies have also reserved rights in certain other specific areas. These were laid out in the Declaration on Berlin Governing Relations Between the Allied (Western) Kommandatura and Berlin, Issued by the Three Western Commandants, which forms part of a package of agreements signed in Bonn on May 26, 1952 (see doc. B5).[28] This agreement had to be reinstituted separately in May 1955 after the Bonn accords were nullified following the French Parliament's rejection of the centerpiece treaty establishing a European Defence Community (EDC). In addition to declaring that the "Allied authorities retain the right to take, if they deem it necessary, such measures as may be required to fulfill their international obligations, to ensure public order, and to maintain the status and security of Berlin and its economy, trade and communications," the three powers stated that they would normally only exercise their rights in the following fields: security, disarmament and demilitarization, representation of Berlin in foreign relations, satisfaction of occupation costs, and control over the local police. As a result of this statute, the Western allies have maintained Berlin's demilitarized status by denying German armed forces access to the city. Thus the presence of East German forces and the establishment of the GDR's Ministry of Defense in East Berlin were always seen by the Western allies as a violation of allied agreements. Arms-related industry and weapon production is similarly banned in West Berlin. Although the allies do very little to involve themselves in the daily activities of the Berlin police, they do continue to reserve the right to approve senior appointments and the purchase of automatic weapons.[29] They have also intervened in public security matters on several occasions. For example, in the wake of the 1986 bombing of a Berlin discotheque, the allied authorities ordered the police to search travelers between East and West Berlin.

Finally, by virtue of its geographic position, Berlin has long been a major center for Western intelligence-gathering on the activities of the Warsaw Pact. While the statutory basis (if any) for Western intelligence operations in Berlin is not publicly known, it has been reported that the U.S. Army Special Operations Field Office located in the city does enjoy the right to intercept mail between East and West Berlin and also eavesdrop on telephone communications.[30]

Although occasional disputes occur between the Western allies and the Soviet Union in the administration of Berlin, the level of friction was dramatically reduced with the Quadripartite Agreement on Berlin and the Final Quadripartite Protocol on Berlin, signed in Berlin on September 3, 1971, and June 3, 1972, respectively (see docs. A11 and A12).[31] Neither agreement altered the rights of the allies in Berlin.[32]

Following unification, allied forces will continue to be stationed in Berlin at the request of the German government but only for as long as Soviet forces remain in the former GDR. The statutory basis for their presence will be negotiated in separate agreements with the relevant governments. Under the terms of the Kohl-Gorbachev agreement German territorial units will also now be allowed into the city.

The Presence of Foreign Forces

As in most other cases, the current rights of the four powers to station forces in Germany can be traced back to the agreements signed immediately after the Second World War. Other than what is implied in the various occupation protocols, the first explicit reference to allied stationing rights can be found in the 1945 declaration of the victorious powers in Berlin (doc. A5). Article 12 states: "The Allied Representatives will station forces and civil agencies in any or all parts of Germany as they may determine." Besides the arrangements permitting U.S., Soviet, British, and French forces in Berlin, no other *quadripartite* agreement on the stationing of troops in Germany evidently exists. These rights rest almost exclusively on miscellaneous tripartite, NATO, and bilateral agreements with the two German states. The four powers, however, on the basis of bilateral agreements among themselves, did establish the right for their military liaison missions in Germany to unimpeded access and freedom of movement ("except places of disposition of military units") in their respective zones of occupation (see doc. D1).[33] Though intended to facilitate cooperation between the occupying forces, the military liaison missions are now used essentially to gather intelligence.

Following the nine-power conference in London in September 1954, which finalized the conditions under which the Federal Republic would become a member of the Brussels Treaty (Western European Union) and with it NATO (see below), representatives of the three main Western powers and the FRG met again in Paris in October 1954 to sign a package of agreements that among other things redefined their right to station forces on German soil. Some of these agreements had originated in the accords signed at Bonn in 1952, which, as noted

9

earlier, never entered into force owing to the failure to gain French parliamentary approval for the European Defence Community treaty. In the Convention on Relations Between the Three Powers and the Federal Republic of Germany, May 26, 1952, As Amended by Schedule I of the Protocol on Termination of the Occupation Regime in Germany (often called the "Relations Convention" or the German Treaty [*Deutschland Vertrag*] by the West Germans), signed on October 23, 1954 (see doc. B3), article 4, para. 1 states that the "Three Powers retain the rights, heretofore exercised or held by them, relating to the stationing of armed forces in the Federal Republic." [34] Given that the central objective of this treaty was to grant the Federal Republic "full authority of a sovereign state over its internal affairs" (article 1, para. 2), it was also agreed that the rights and obligations of these forces would henceforth be governed by a separate Convention on the Rights and Obligations of Foreign Forces and Their Members in the Federal Republic of Germany (known as the "Forces Convention").[35] This, however, was only to stay in force until the Federal Republic acceded to the standard contractual arrangements reached for other NATO countries. Thus, the "Forces Convention" was subsequently repealed with the FRG's signing of the Agreement Between the Parties to the North Atlantic Treaty Regarding the Status of Their Forces, widely known as the "Status of Forces" agreement.[36] This was signed along with several supplementary agreements on August 3, 1959.

In acceding to the NATO Status of Forces agreement, the Federal Republic agreed to accept certain rights for foreign forces on its soil.[37] These cover such diverse issues as personal identification and civil registration, criminal jurisdiction, property laws, civil court proceedings and arbitration, freedom of movement, the right to bear arms, aerial photography, training maneuvers (in the air and on land), compensation for maneuver damage, accommodation, taxation and customs, postal service, telecommunications, and radio/TV broadcasting. Since 1959 this agreement has been periodically reviewed and revised.

While the overall intent of the "Relations Convention" was to end the occupation regime, grant full sovereignty to the Federal Republic, and, furthermore, normalize the role and presence of foreign forces in West Germany, the three Western powers were careful to draw the distinction in article 4, para. 2, between their right to station forces *in the Federal Republic* and their right to do the same *in Germany*. Whereas the purpose of the forces in the first case is "defence of the free world, of which Berlin and the Federal Republic form part," in the second it is to uphold their quadripartite rights and responsibilities relating to "Berlin and to Germany as a whole, including the reunification of Germany and a peace settlement." The same section also grants that "forces of the same nationality and effective strength" at the time the FRG becomes a member of NATO "may be stationed in the Federal Republic."

10

This right was reiterated in yet another agreement signed at Paris on October 23, 1954, the Convention on the Presence of Foreign Forces in the Federal Republic of Germany (doc. B6).[38] Although the precise meaning of "effective strength" was never defined, this convention did stipulate that the deployment of additional forces, including those for training (which can stay only for thirty days), would require the consent of the FRG government. American, British, and French forces, however, do not require governmental approval to enter, pass through, and depart the FRG in transit to any other member state of NATO. Since France decided in 1966 to leave NATO's integrated military command, the legal basis for the presence of its forces in West Germany required some change.[39] As a result, the two countries reached an Understanding on the Right of Stationing and the Questions Relating to Status of the French Forces in Germany, which was signed on December 21, 1966.[40]

It is important to note here that certain other stationing rights evidently remain in effect from the "Relations Convention" that are not stated in other agreements. Paragraph 2 of article 5 states:

The rights of the Three powers, heretofore held or exercised by them, which relate to the protection of the security of armed forces stationed in the Federal Republic and which are temporarily retained, shall lapse when the appropriate German authorities have obtained similar powers under German legislation enabling them to take effective action to protect the security of those forces, including the ability to deal with a serious disturbance of public security and order. To the extent that such rights continue to be exercisable they shall be exercised only after consultation, insofar as the military situation does not preclude such consultation, with the Federal Government and with its agreement that the circumstances require such exercise. In all other respects the protection of the security of those forces shall be governed by the Forces Convention.

The clause giving emergency rights to the allied forces in the event of internal threats to their security was revoked in 1968 following the amendments to the Basic Law that turned responsibility for ensuring the safety of allied troops over to German domestic authorities.[41] These changes, however, did not alter the general right for military commanders to take emergency measures to protect their forces against other threats. This understanding was acknowledged by Konrad Adenauer in a letter sent to the three allied powers in 1954.[42] And it was reiterated by Secretary of State John Foster Dulles in his report to President Eisenhower on November 12, 1954: "The termination of the general right of the three powers in this field [i.e. security of their forces] will not affect the right of a military commander, if his forces are imminently menaced, to take such immediate action

11

(including the use of armed force) as may be appropriate for their protection and as is requisite to remove the danger."[43]

American forces stationed in the Federal Republic evidently also enjoy special rights in the event that a nuclear weapon–related accident occurs.[44] While this agreement remains classified, some indication of the associated powers surfaced when a U.S. A-10 jet aircraft crashed into the town of Remscheid, near Dusseldorf, in 1988. Local German authorities were reportedly excluded from the crash site by U.S. military personnel.[45]

The Soviet Union and the German Democratic Republic also made special arrangements for stationing Soviet forces on German soil. In the Statement by the Soviet Union Attributing Full Sovereignty to the German Democratic Republic (doc. D2) reference was made to the "temporary stationing of Soviet troops on the territory of the German Democratic Republic." [46] Article 4 of the subsequent Treaty on Relations Between the Soviet Union and the German Democratic Republic, signed in Moscow on September 20, 1955 (doc. D3), explicitly states:

> The Soviet forces now stationed in the territory of the German Democratic Republic in accordance with existing international agreements shall temporarily remain in the German Democratic Republic, with the consent of its Government and subject to conditions which shall be defined in a supplementary agreement between the Government of the Soviet Union and the Government of the German Democratic Republic.

While this same article also specifies that Soviet forces would not intervene in the domestic affairs or social and political life of the GDR, the bilateral Status of Forces agreement between the two countries "implicitly grants Soviets the authority to impose a state of emergency on the GDR in response to internal or external conditions." [47] And, like the Western allied arrangements in the FRG, this agreement contains an emergency clause that "in the event of a threat to the security of Soviet forces" in the GDR, the supreme commander of the Group of Soviet Forces in Germany (GSFG), after consultation with the GDR government, "can take measures for the elimination of such a threat." This agreement, furthermore, does not accord the East Germans any rights with regard to the number and disposition of Soviet forces in their country.[48]

III: Legal Constraints on German Military Power

The extant legal constraints on German military power affect the circumstances in which force can be legitimately used, the size and structure of

Germany's armed forces, political and military command relationships, and weapon production rights. Each will be discussed in turn.

The Use of Force

The most important legal limits to the use of force are contained in the 1949 Basic Law (*Grundgesetz*) creating the Federal Republic. This declares "unconstitutional" any "Activities tending to disturb, and undertaken with the intention of disturbing, the peaceful relations between nations, especially of preparing the conduct of an aggressive war." [49] With the establishment of the West German armed forces in 1955, the Basic Law was amended by article 87(a) to specify that the Federal Republic could build up and use its armed forces for defensive purposes only. This has been widely interpreted to preclude any deployment or use of armed force that is not for territorial defense. The same article, however, does specify that exceptions can be made, but only to the extent permitted by the Basic Law. In this context constitutional lawyers point to article 24, which states that "For the maintenance of peace, the Federation may join a system of mutual collective security; in doing so it will consent to those limitations of its sovereign powers which will bring about and secure a peaceful and lasting order, in Europe and among the nations of the world." Some have interpreted this as meaning that the Federal Republic can participate in U.N. peacekeeping operations.[50] While there have been periodic initiatives to make the constitution less restrictive on the use of German armed forces—most recently with the Persian Gulf crisis—the predominant sentiment has been to keep it as presently worded. For reference, the relevant articles have been reproduced in appendix E.

Besides the Basic Law, the Federal Republic has at various times made declarations and entered into agreements that also circumscribe the instances in which force can be used legitimately. At the completion of the nine-power conference in London, which set the terms for the Federal Republic's membership in the Brussels Treaty and the North Atlantic Treaty, the government of the FRG issued the declaration stating that not only that it would observe the obligations set forth in article 2 of the U.N. Charter—namely that all international disputes should be settled peacefully and that states should refrain from the threat or use of force against the territorial integrity or political independence of other states—but also that it would "refrain from any action inconsistent with the strictly defensive character" of both treaties. More particularly, "the German Federal Republic undertakes never to have recourse to force to achieve the reunification of Germany or the modification of the present boundaries of the German Federal Republic, and to resolve by peaceful means any disputes which may arise between the Federal Republic and other States" (see doc. C1).[51]

13

Virtually identical language was used in the Protocol to the North Atlantic Treaty on the Accession of the Federal Republic of Germany, which was signed at Paris on October 23, 1954 (see doc. C2).[52]

Likewise, in the Warsaw, Moscow, and Prague Treaties between the FRG and Poland, the Soviet Union, and Czechoslovakia, respectively, the use of force to settle international disputes or change existing territorial boundaries was formally renounced.[53] Finally, both the FRG and the GDR have signed the Helsinki Final Act of 1975, which contains very similar undertakings (doc. C5).[54] This same agreement also constrains the size of military maneuvers and imposes certain advance notification requirements for all thirty-five state signatories as a general confidence-building measure.

The Size and Structure of German Military Forces

The size and structure of the Federal Republic's armed forces in peacetime was originally set by the Special Agreement annexed to the 1952 treaty establishing the European Defence Community. As described earlier, the EDC initiative ultimately failed, but the agreed limits on West Germany's military contribution to the defense of Western Europe were later incorporated into the terms of its membership in the Western European Union (the Brussels Treaty) and, with it, NATO. This is laid down in the Protocol No. II on Forces of Western European Union, signed in Paris on October 23, 1954 (see doc. C3).[55] The original Special Agreement has never been released to the public, but the general nature of the limits on the German defense contribution is widely known. A peacetime ceiling of 500,000 men was set for the Bundeswehr, of which approximately 310,100 men would make up an army organized into 12 divisions (6 armored and 6 mechanized infantry). An air force consisting of 1,326 tactical aircraft would also be allowed as well as a navy of 186 light coastal defense/escort vessels and 54 aircraft.[56] The same protocol permits states to increase their forces above the agreed ceilings—explicitly in the case of naval forces and implicitly for others—but only on the recommendations of NATO's military authorities and, moreover, with the unanimous consent of the "High Contracting Parties." The supreme allied commander, Europe (SACEUR) was also made responsible for monitoring compliance with the agreed limitations. Other than the stipulation that the "naval forces of the Federal Republic shall consist of the vessels and formations necessary for the defensive missions assigned to it by the North Atlantic Treaty Organization," there are no specific constraints in this protocol on the deployment or employment of West Germany's military forces.

While the Federal Republic continues to observe the overall manpower limit of 500,000 men, this does not include the mobilizable reserves and a cadre Home

Defense force that remains under national command in wartime.[57] Certain equipment constraints, particularly for naval forces, have evidently also been lifted since the protocol was signed.

Political and Military Command Relationships

It is frequently stated or, at least, inferred that the armed forces of West Germany have a qualitatively different relationship to NATO's integrated military command from that of other members of the alliance. More particularly, the Bundeswehr is committed exclusively to the NATO defense mission, as described above, and SACEUR maintains operational control over its military activities in peacetime. The combined effect of these two provisions, therefore, is that West Germany has little or no latitude for independent military initiative. The reality, however, is somewhat different.

Under the original terms for West German rearmament and the creation of the Bundeswehr, it was agreed, largely at the insistence of France, that the Federal Republic's military forces would form part of a European army under supranational allied command. With the demise of the EDC initiative, however, new means to assuage France's concerns over German rearmament and gain its acquiescence to the Federal Republic's membership of the Western European Union and ultimately NATO had to be found. The solution, as agreed at the London nine-power conference in September 1954, was to strengthen NATO's embryonic military command structure, especially the responsibilities and authority of SACEUR, and commit West Germany's armed forces to it.[58] The idea, in essence, was to make Europe's armed forces and West Germany's so integrated and interdependent as to preclude "nationalistic adventures."[59]

As a result, under Protocol II on Forces of Western European Union (doc. C3), the High Contracting Parties agreed to "place under the Supreme Allied Commander, Europe, in peacetime on the mainland of Europe" land and air forces up to the stipulated maximums. In a separate resolution of the North Atlantic Council that was passed on October 22, 1954 (doc. C4), NATO members further agreed that "all the forces of member nations stationed in the area of Allied Command Europe shall be placed under the authority of the Supreme Allied Commander Europe or other appropriate NATO command and under the direction of the NATO military authorities with the exception of those forces intended for the defense of overseas territories *and other forces which the North Atlantic Treaty Organization has recognised or will recognise as suitable to remain under national command.*"[60] As a result of this vital caveat and in contrast to the apparent meaning of these agreements, the vast majority of NATO's forces remain under national control in peacetime. While each nation

15

has designated or "assigned" certain forces to NATO in the event of an emergency, national command authority must be formally transferred with government approval (or "chopped" in the jargon) to NATO. SACEUR, therefore, has no real operational control over the forces assigned to him in peacetime except for the U.S. forces under his command as commander-in-chief, Europe (CINCEUR), some small special purpose NATO multinational units, and NATO's air defense interceptor aircraft.[61]

Other than the exclusive commitment of the Bundeswehr to the defense of NATO, the status of West Germany's armed forces within the integrated military command is evidently no different from that of any other alliance member.[62] As the 1985 West German *White Paper* on defense policy categorically states:

> In a period of crisis, at the latest upon the promulgation of a state of defense, the Federal Republic of Germany will transfer, *by decision of the Federal Republic,* operational command over all NATO-assigned German forces to the NATO commanders. Such transfer of operational command is, as is NATO assignment of German forces in peacetime, based on the sovereign decision of the Federal Republic of Germany. It becomes effective upon release of specific measures of the NATO Alert System. The implementation of these measures is again *subject to the sovereign decision of the Federal Government.*[63]

Similarly, as a 1955 U.S. Senate Foreign Relations Report states:

> Under the provisions of articles V and XI of the North Atlantic Treaty, to which the Federal Republic will now be a party, the engagement of forces in combat is a matter for national decision in accordance with the respective constitutional processes of the parties. The supreme allied commander in Europe (SACEUR) would have no authority to engage the forces of any nation in hostilities until the nation concerned had determined that it wished to take such action under article V of the North Atlantic Treaty.[64]

The only German units that SACEUR could order to engage in hostilities are its air defense forces. Conversely, there are no NATO or allied constraints on the Federal Republic's freedom to mobilize its armed forces in a national emergency. Furthermore, West Germany's sizable Territorial Home Defense force is not formally committed to NATO and would remain under national control even in wartime.[65]

It is important to note here that there are constitutional checks and balances in the Federal Republic against the abuse of its military power. In peacetime, the minister of defense has been vested with command over the armed forces, which is transferred to the federal chancellor during wartime or a grave emergency. The old General Staff system no longer exists. In fact the chief of staff of the Bundeswehr is not even in the chain of command and therefore has no operational control over West Germany's forces.[66] For these forces to be committed to military action requires parliamentary approval and the declaration of a state of tension and a state of defense (*Verteidigungsfall*).[67] If both chambers of Parliament (Bundesrat and Bundestag) are unable to convene in time or if the necessary quorum is not achieved, then a Joint Committee, made up of twenty-two members of all parties under the chairmanship of the Bundestag's president, will then act on its behalf.[68]

In contrast to the Federal Republic's virtual sovereignty over its armed forces, the National Peoples Army (NVA) of the GDR has remained subordinate to Soviet control in one form or another since its evolution from a paramilitary police force in 1956.[69] Whereas the armed forces of other Warsaw Pact countries eventually gained some independence—though never complete—the NVA has remained under the strict supervision of Soviet authorities and, in particular, the GSFG (now Western Group of Soviet Forces). It is "the only East European military establishment wholly subordinated to Warsaw Pact Command in peacetime." [70] This was illustrated in November 1989 when Soviet authorities reportedly played a significant role in dissuading East German forces from being used to put down the civil unrest that preceded the fall of the Berlin Wall and the end of the Erich Honecker regime.[71] Given the nature of the subsequent political changes in the GDR, this may have been the last time that the Soviet Union enjoyed such influence with the GDR military.

Weapon Production Rights

Both the FRG and the GDR have accepted constraints on their freedom to develop and produce certain types of weaponry. In 1954, as part of the conditions for West Germany's rearmament, the then federal chancellor, Konrad Adenauer, made the binding declaration that

> The Federal Republic undertakes not to manufacture in its territory any atomic weapons ... defined as any weapon which contains ... nuclear fuel ... is capable of mass destruction ... [or] any part, device, assembly or material especially designed for ... any [such] weapons.[72]

17

As Soviet and other commentators have since observed, this pledge did not prevent West Germany from acquiring nuclear weapons from other states or from entering into co-ownership arrangements with others. Neither did it prevent the Federal Republic from developing and manufacturing nuclear weapons outside its own territory.[73] At the time, it was also understood by Adenauer and by the U.S. secretary of state, John Foster Dulles, that the declaration was binding only *rebus sic stantibus,* that is, while existing conditions prevailed.[74] In the meantime, however, the FRG and the GDR have each signed the 1963 Partial Test Ban Treaty prohibiting atmospheric nuclear testing and the 1968 Treaty on the Non-Proliferation of Nuclear Weapons. Article II of the latter states:

> Each non-nuclear weapon State Party to the Treaty undertakes not to receive the transfer from any transferor whatsoever of nuclear weapons or other nuclear explosive devices or of control over such weapons or explosive devices directly, or indirectly; not to manufacture or otherwise acquire nuclear weapons or other nuclear explosive devices; and not to seek or receive assistance in the manufacture of nuclear weapons or other nuclear devices.[75]

While this apparently covers many of the omissions of the Federal Republic's earlier nonproliferation pledge, parties to the agreement nevertheless retain the sovereign right in the event that "extraordinary events" jeopardize their "supreme interests," to withdraw with three months' notice from the NPT Treaty (article X).

In addition to renouncing the manufacture of atomic weapons as part of its accession to the WEU, the Federal Republic included biological and chemical weapons in the same pledge (see doc. C1).[76] It also agreed to specific limitations on a sizable list of conventional weapons along with inspection and verification arrangements to be administered by the WEU's Agency for the Control of Armaments. Although the restrictions on atomic, biological, and chemical weapon production remain in force, the limitations on conventional weapons were lifted in their entirety on January 1, 1986.[77]

IV: Conclusion

The "Final Settlement" document on Germany, as noted earlier, will formally terminate the quadripartite rights relating to German unification, territorial borders, and Berlin. The allies' right to base forces on German soil as part of their *quadripartite* responsibilities will no doubt also lapse. This leaves, however, other arrangements in effect that are likely to become the subject of separate negotiations. These affect the future role, if any, for the allied military liaison missions; the right to conduct intelligence operations from German soil, especially Berlin; the protection of German airspace; civil-military relations in the event of nuclear accidents; and allied basing rights in general. Many of these arrangements were already becoming an issue of public debate in West Germany before the unification process started. As Germany regains its full sovereignty, they are sure to attract even more public attention.

As suggested in the introduction to this study, many of the functions performed by the existing legal constraints on German military power can be subsumed into wider pan-European arrangements. For example, the size of the German armed forces will become part of the Conventional Forces in Europe agreement. The exercise and movement of these forces will likewise be covered by CSBM restrictions that apply to all thirty-five nations of the Conference on Security and Cooperation in Europe. Other arrangements could be applied to military air operations in Europe. The Berlin Air Safety Center, for instance, provides the nucleus for a European airspace management system, something that will be essential while Soviet airplanes remain in East Germany. It has also been suggested that Berlin be the location for a new European crisis management center. Overall, such initiatives provide the most productive way to dispel fears about Germany's military potential and provide a solid basis for ensuring long-term peace and security in Europe.

Notes

1. For the text of the joint German-Soviet "Communiqué" and excerpts of the associated press conference, see "Excerpts from Kohl-Gorbachev News Conference," *New York Times,* July 17, 1990, p. A8.

2. "Testimony of Michael K. Young, Deputy Legal Adviser, U.S. Department of State, before the Senate Foreign Relations Committee on the Legal Aspects of German Unification," July 12, 1990, p. 9.

3. See Marc Fisher, "Kohl Seeks German Role in a U.N. Force in Gulf," *Washington Post,* August 17, 1990, p. A16.

4. A very useful review, however, is Raymond J. Celada, "German Reunification: United States Reserved or Retained Rights," prepared for the Senate Committee on Foreign Relations, *Legal Issues Relating to the Future Status of Germany,* 101 Cong. 2d sess. (Government Printing Office, 1990), pp. 1–8.

5. The former allied powers, however, did formally terminate a state of war with Germany: Britain, France, and the United States in 1951 and the Soviet Union in 1955.

6. For the full text see U.S. Department of State, *Documents on Germany, 1944–1985,* pp. 1–3. (Hereafter *DoG*.)

7. The original protocol has been amended twice. The first time was by the Agreement Amending the Protocol on Zones of Occupation in Germany and Administration of the "Greater Berlin" Area, Approved by the European Advisory Commission, November 14, 1944 (see doc. A2), in *DoG*, pp. 4–5. This gave U.S. military authorities use of ports at Bremen and Bremerhaven in addition to transit rights through the British zone. The second time was by the Agreement Further Amending the Protocol of September 12, 1944 To Include France in the Occupation of Germany and Administration of "Greater Berlin," Approved by the European Advisory Commission, July 26, 1945 (see doc. A3), in *DoG*, pp. 44–48.

8. *DoG*, pp. 6–9.

9. France subsequently became a party to this arrangement in the Agreement Amending the Agreement on Control Machinery in Germany to Provide for the Participation of France, Adopted by the European Advisory Commission, May 1, 1945, in *DoG*, pp. 12–13.

10. *DoG*, pp. 33–38.

11. *DoG*, pp. 54–65.

12. See the following: doc. B1: Basic Principles for Merger of the Three Western German Zones of Occupation and Creation of an Allied High Commission, Signed at Washington, April 8, 1949, in *DoG*, pp. 215–56; doc. B2: Occupation Statute Defining the Powers To Be Retained by the Occupation Authorities, Signed by the Three Western Foreign Ministers, April 8, 1949, in *DoG*, pp. 212–14; and doc. B3: Convention on Relations Between the Three Powers and the Federal Republic of Germany, May 26, 1952, As Amended by Schedule I of the Protocol on Termination of the Occupation Regime in Germany, Signed at Paris, October 23, 1954, in *DoG*, pp. 425–30.

13. See doc. D2: Statement by the Soviet Union Attributing Full Sovereignty to the German Democratic Republic, March 25, 1954, in *DoG*, pp. 418–19; doc. D4: Soviet–East German Treaty on Friendship, Mutual Assistance, and Cooperation, Signed at

Moscow, June 12, 1964, in *DoG,* pp. 869–72. See especially article II. See also in response to the latter agreement in the Declaration Issued by France, the United Kingdom, and the United States Concerning the Soviet–East German Friendship Treaty, June 26, 1964, in *DoG,* pp. 877–78.

14. At the same time, the former German city of Koenigsberg and the area adjacent to it (now the Kaliningrad Oblast of the Russian Soviet Federated Socialist Republic) would be ceded to the Soviet Union "pending final determination of territorial questions at the peace settlement."

15. For example, the Convention on Relations Between the Three Powers and the Federal Republic of Germany, May 26, 1952, As Amended by Schedule I of the Protocol on Termination of the Occupation Regime in Germany, Signed at Paris, October 23, 1954 (see doc. B3) includes the statement in article 7 that "the final determination of the boundaries of Germany" must await a peace settlement. *DoG,* pp. 427–28.

16. Article 6 of chapter 12. See *DoG,* p. 431.

17. This came to light recently when a Polish MiG-23 flying on automatic control strayed into West Germany after its pilot had ejected soon after takeoff. See Ian Kemp, "How Did Pilotless 'Flogger' Escape WP?" *Jane's Defense Weekly,* July 15, 1989, p. 61. See also Peter Almond, "Stray MiG Incident Prompts Talk of Military Hotline," *Washington Times,* July 6, 1989, p. 11.

18. Interview. The two officers are most probably the commander-in-chief of RAF Germany and the commander-in-chief of U.S. Air Forces Europe.

19. This arrangement was subsequently reaffirmed by article 7 of the Agreement on Control Machinery (doc. A4). The allied right to supreme authority over Berlin also implicitly derives from the Berlin Declaration of the victorious powers (doc. A5). See also agreements reprinted in *DoG,* pp. 38–39, 43–44.

20. Notes of a Conference Among Marshal Zhukov, General Clay, and General Weeks on Surface and Air Access to Berlin, June 29, 1945 (doc. A7), in *DoG,* pp. 42–43.

21. *DoG,* pp. 72–74.

22. *DoG,* pp. 99–109.

23. Four-Power Communiqué on Arrangements for Lifting the Berlin Blockade Effective May 12, New York, May 4, 1949, in *DoG,* p. 221. See also Order Number 56 of the Soviet Military Administration in Germany Lifting the Berlin Blockade May 12, Issued May 9, 1949, in *DoG,* pp. 258–60.

24. With the death of Rudolf Hess, its last inmate, the Spandau prison was torn down in 1987.

25. See Letter From the Military Governors of the Three Western Zones of Occupation to the President of the West German Parliamentary Council Approving, With Reservations, the Basic Law for the Federal Republic, May 12, 1949, in *DoG,* pp. 260–62; and Letter From the Allied (Western) Kommandatura to the West Berlin Authorities Approving, With Reservations, the West Berlin Constitution, August 29, 1950, in *DoG,* pp. 340–41.

26. Letter From the Allied (Western) Kommandatura to the Mayor of Berlin Regarding Inclusion of Berlin in International Undertakings of the Federal Republic, May 21, 1952, in *DoG,* pp. 372–74.

27. See Richard C. Hottelet, "Berlin's Fate Still Tied to the 'Four Powers,'" *Christian Science Monitor,* October 13, 1989, p. 19. The Soviets recognize this right and do

the same in return. These patrols should not be confused with the activities of the military liaison missions, which are discussed below.

28. *DoG*, pp. 379–82.

29. See Ray Mosely, "In West Berlin, Allies Call Shots," *Chicago Tribune,* November 30, 1989, p. 5.

30. See Jeffrey T. Richelson, *The U.S. Intelligence Community,* 2d ed. (Ballinger, 1989), p. 258.

31. *DoG*, pp. 1135–43, 1204–06.

32. See Address by Ambassador Rush Discussing the Quadripartite Agreement, September 27, 1971, in *DoG,* pp. 1155–67.

33. Agreement Between the Military Liaison Missions Accredited to the Soviet and United States Commanders-in-Chief of the Zones of Occupation In Germany, April 5, 1947, in *DoG,* pp. 114–15. Similar agreements were reached between the the Soviet Union, Britain, and France.

34. *DoG*, pp. 425–30.

35. Signed May 26, 1952, amended by protocol of October 23, 1954. For the complete text see *American Foreign Policy, 1950–1955* (U.S. Department of State, 1957), pp. 498–539.

36. This was originally signed at London on June 19,1951. For the full text see ibid., pp. 1529–44.

37. For the complete text with supplementary agreements see U.S. Department of State, *U.S. Treaties and Other International Agreements,* vol. 1, pt. 1 (1963), pp. 537–685.

38. See *American Foreign Policy, 1950–1955*, pp. 610–12.

39. For background see *DoG*, pp. 919–21, 924–27.

40. Federal Ministry of Defence, *White Paper 1985: The Situation and the Development of the Federal Armed Services* (1985), p. 69.

41. See Dennis L. Bark and David R. Gress, *From Shadow to Substance, 1945–1963* (Cambridge: Basil Blackwell, 1989), p. 333. For historical background on this issue see U.S. Department of State, *Foreign Relations of the United States, 1952–1954,* vol. 7: *Germany and Austria,* pt. 1 (1986), pp. 21–22, 28–30, 55–56. See also vol. 5: *Western European Security* (1983), pt. 2, p. 1168, of the same series.

42. See Beate Ruhm von Oppen, ed., *Documents on Germany under Occupation, 1945–1954* (Oxford University Press, 1955), p. 628.

43. See "Report by the Secretary of State to the President, November 12, 1954," in *American Foreign Policy, 1950–1955,* p. 616.

44. Confidential interview with author.

45. Serge Schemann, "U.S. Plane Crashes into German City," *New York Times,* December 9, 1988, p. 7; and "West Germans Say the U.S. Hampered Air Crash Rescue," *New York Times,* December 10, 1988, p. 28.

46. *DoG*, p. 459.

47. Quoted from Douglas A. Macgregor, "The GDR: A Model Mobilization," in Jeffrey Simon, ed., *NATO–Warsaw Pact Force Mobilization* (National Defense University Press, 1988), p. 191.

48. A. Ross Johnson, Robert W. Dean, and Alexander Alexiev, *East European Military Establishments: The Warsaw Pact Northern Tier,* R-2417/1-AF/FF (Santa Monica, Calif.: Rand Corporation, 1980), p. 82.

49. For the text of the Basic Law see *The Basic Law of The Federal Republic of Germany* (Bonn: Press and Information Office of the Federal Government, 1986).

50. In 1989 the West German government sent a small contingent of its special Border forces *(Bundesgrenzshutz)*, which are not part of the Bundeswehr, to Namibia for peacekeeping purposes.

51. *DoG*, p. 422.

52. *DoG*, p. 432.

53. See *DoG*, pp. 1103–05, 1125–27, 1256–58.

54. *DoG*, pp. 1285–96.

55. See *American Foreign Policy, 1950–1955*, pp. 977–79.

56. See von Oppen, ed., *Documents under Occupation*, p. 639; and Bark and Gress, *From Shadow to Substance*, p. 290.

57. The latter may be permitted under a separate provision of the WEU protocol that allows the strength and armaments of "internal defence and police forces" to be fixed by separate agreement.

58. For interesting background reading see Department of State, *Foreign Relations of the United States, 1952–1954*, vol. 5, pt. 2, pp. 1281–82, 1294–1366.

59. Ibid., p. 1381. See also p. 1475.

60. See Resolution to Implement Section IV of the Final Act of the London Conference, in ibid., pp. 1431–34 (emphasis added). This resolution also lays out how SACEUR's authority was to be expanded and enlarged.

61. See General Wolfgang Altenburg, "Defense in the Air-NATO's Integrated Air Defense Today and in the Future," *NATO's Sixteen Nations*, August 1986, p. 23.

62. See Federal Ministry of Defence, *White Paper 1985*, pp. 111, 169.

63. Ibid., p. 170 (emphasis added).

64. *American Foreign Policy, 1950–1955*, p. 637.

65. Ibid., p. 171.

66. See Catherine McArdle Kelleher, "Defense Organization in Germany: A Twice Told Tale," in Robert J. Art, Vincent Davis, and Samuel P. Huntington, eds., *Reorganizing America's Defense: Leadership in War and Peace* (Pergamon-Brassey, 1985), p. 83. The chief of staff essentially acts as the executive agent for the minister of defense.

67. The defense minister, however, has the discretionary authority to call up some reserves to "standby readiness."

68. *White Paper 1985*, pp. 163–69. See also article 115 of the Basic Law, which is more specific about parliamentary powers in a state of defense. This has been reproduced in appendix E.

69. Macgregor, "The GDR: A Model Mobilization," pp. 190–94.

70. Johnson and others, *East European Military Establishments*, p. 82; see also note 15, p. 123.

71. See "Interview with East German Defense Minister," *Radio Free Europe/ Radio Liberty Daily Report*, no. 130 (July 11, 1990), p. 2.

72. Quoted from Catherine McArdle Kelleher, *Germany and the Politics of Nuclear Weapons* (Columbia University Press, 1985), p. 9, and combines the language of Annex 1 and Annex II of Protocol No III of the Brussels Treaty On the Control of Armaments, Signed in Paris on October 23, 1954. For full text see *American Foreign Policy, 1950–1955*, pp. 980–81.

73. Kelleher, *Germany and the Politics of Nuclear Weapons*, p. 9.

74. Ibid., pp. 10, 26, 30.

75. U.S. Arms Control and Disarmament Agency, *Arms Control and Disarmament Agreements: Texts and Histories of Negotiations,* 1980 ed., p. 91.

76. Both the FRG and the GDR are also party to the 1972 Biological Weapons Convention.

77. Statement by Western European Union Foreign and Defence Ministers on Institutional Reform, Rome, October 27, 1984, in *DoG,* pp. 1379–80. It is worth noting that the Soviet authorities in the GDR evidently maintained strict controls on East German weapon production. See Johnson and others, *East European Military Establishments,* p. 82.

Appendix A. Quadripartite Agreements

A1. Protocol on Zones of Occupation in Germany and Administration of the "Greater Berlin" Area, Approved by the European Advisory Commission, September 12, 1944

A2. Agreement Amending the Protocol on Zones of Occupation in Germany and Administration of the "Greater Berlin" Area, Approved by the European Advisory Commission, November 14, 1944

A3. Agreement Further Amending the Protocol of September 12, 1944 To Include France in the Occupation of Germany and Administration of "Greater Berlin," Approved by the European Advisory Commission, July 26, 1945

A4. Agreement on Control Machinery in Germany, Adopted by the European Advisory Commission, November 14, 1944

A5. Declaration Regarding the Defeat of Germany and the Assumption of Supreme Authority by the Allied Powers, Signed at Berlin, June 5, 1945

A6. Protocol of the Proceedings of the Berlin (Potsdam) Conference, August 1, 1945

A7. Notes of a Conference Among Marshal Zhukov, General Clay, and General Weeks on Surface and Air Access to Berlin, June 29, 1945

A8. Decision of the Control Council Approving Establishment of Berlin–Hamburg, Berlin–Buckeburg (Hannover), and Berlin–Frankfurt-am-Main Air Corridors, November 30, 1945

A9. Revised Regulations Governing Flights in Air Corridors in Germany and the Berlin Control Zone, Issued by the Air Directorate, October 22, 1946

A10. Four-Power Communiqué on Arrangements for Lifting the Berlin Blockade Effective May 12, New York, May 4, 1949

A11. Quadripartite Agreement on Berlin, Signed at Berlin, September 3, 1971

A12. Final Quadripartite Protocol on Berlin, Signed at Berlin, June 3, 1972

Document A1

Protocol on Zones of Occupation in Germany and Administration of the "Greater Berlin" Area, Approved by the European Advisory Commission, September 12, 1944 [1]

The Governments of the United States of America, the United Kingdom of Great Britain and Northern Ireland, and the Union of Soviet Socialist Republics have reached the following agreement with regard to the execution of Article 11 of the Instrument of Unconditional Surrender of Germany: [2]—

1. Germany, within her frontiers as they were on the 31st December, 1937, will, for the purposes of occupation, be divided into three zones, one of which will be allotted to each of the three Powers, and a special Berlin area, which will be under joint occupation by the three Powers.

2. The boundaries of the three zones and of the Berlin area, and the allocation of the three zones as between the U.S.A., the U.K. and the U.S.S.R. will be as follows:—

Eastern Zone (as shown on the annexed map "A" [3])

The territory of Germany (including the province of East Prussia) situated to the East of a line drawn from the point on Lübeck Bay where the frontiers of Schleswig-Holstein and Mecklenburg meet, along the western frontier of Mecklenburg to the frontier of the province of Hanover, thence, along the eastern frontier of Hanover, to the frontier of Brunswick; thence along the western frontier of the Prussian province of

---

[1] Treaties and Other International Acts Series 3071. The protocol was approved by the United States on February 2, 1945; the United Kingdom, December 5, 1944; and the Soviet Union, February 6, 1945. The amendment of November 14, 1944 (*post*), allocated the northwestern parts of Germany and Greater Berlin to the United Kingdom, established the Bremen enclave for the United States, and assigned the southwestern part of Germany and the southern part of Berlin to the United States. In accordance with the Yalta Agreement of February 11, 1945 (*post*), this protocol was further amended on July 26, 1945, to provide for French occupation zones, both in Germany and in Greater Berlin (*post*).

[2] I.e., the draft surrender terms agreed upon in the European Advisory Commission on July 25, 1944. The text of this draft instrument appears in *Foreign Relations, The Conferences at Malta and Yalta, 1945*, pp. 113–117. Article 11 read as follows: "The Allied Representatives will station forces and civil agencies in any or all parts of Germany as they may determine." The draft instrument (amended on May 1, 1945, to include France) was not used when Germany actually surrendered, but was incorporated in large part into the Declaration Regarding the Defeat of Germany and the Assumption of Supreme Authority by the Allied Powers, June 5, 1945 (*post*).

[3] Not printed here; see 5 UST 2078.

Saxony to the western frontier of Anhalt, thence along the western frontier of Anhalt; thence along the western frontier of the Prussian province of Saxony and the western frontier of Thuringia to where the latter meets the Bavarian frontier; then eastwards along the northern frontier of Bavaria to the 1937 Czechoslovakian frontier, will be occupied by armed forces of the U.S.S.R., with the exception of the Berlin area, for which a special system of occupation is provided below.

North-Western Zone (as shown on the annexed map "A")

The territory of Germany situated to the west of the line defined above, and bounded on the south by a line drawn from the point where the western frontier of Thuringia meets the frontier of Bavaria; thence westwards along the southern frontiers of the Prussian provinces of Hessen-Nassau and Rheinprovinz to where the latter meets the frontier of France will be occupied by armed forces of . . .

South-Western Zone (as shown on the annexed map "A")

All the remaining territory of Western Germany situated to the south of the line defined in the description of the North-Western Zone will be occupied by armed forces of . . .

The frontiers of States (Länder) and Provinces within Germany, referred to in the foregoing descriptions of the zones, are those which existed after the coming into effect of the decree of 25th June, 1941 (published in the Reichsgesetzblatt, Part I, No. 72, 3rd July, 1941).

Berlin Area (as shown on the annexed 4 sheets of map "B" [4])

The Berlin area (by which expression is understood the territory of "Greater Berlin" as defined by the Law of the 27th April 1920) will be jointly occupied by armed forces of the U.S.A., U.K., and U.S.S.R., assigned by the respective Commanders-in-Chief. For this purpose the territory of "Greater Berlin" will be divided into the following three parts:

North-Eastern part of "Greater Berlin" (districts of Pankow, Prenzlauerberg, Mitte, Weissensee, Fredrichshain, Lichtenberg, Treptow, Köpenick) will be occupied by the forces of the U.S.S.R.:

North-Western part of "Greater Berlin" (districts of Reinickendorf, Wedding, Tiergarten, Charlottenberg, Spandau, Wilmersdorf) will be occupied by the forces of . . .

Southern part of "Greater Berlin" (districts of Zehlendorf, Steglitz, Schöneberg, Kreuzberg, Tempelhof, Neukölln) will be occupied by the forces of . . .

The boundaries of districts within "Greater Berlin", referred to in the foregoing descriptions, are those which existed after the coming into effect of the decree published on 27th March, 1938 (Amtsblatt der Reichshauptstadt Berlin No. 13 of 27th March, 1938, page 215).

3. The occupying forces in each of the three zones into which Germany is divided will be under a Commander-in-Chief desig-

---

[4] Not printed here; see 5 UST 2080.

nated by the Government of the country whose forces occupy that zone.

4. Each of the three Powers may, at its discretion, include among the forces assigned to occupation duties under the command of its Commander-in-Chief, auxiliary contingents from the forces of any other Allied Power which has participated in military operations against Germany.

5. An Inter-Allied Governing Authority (Komendatura) consisting of three Commandants, appointed by their respective Commanders-in-Chief, will be established to direct jointly the administration of the "Greater Berlin" Area.

6. This Protocol has been drawn up in triplicate in the English and Russian languages. Both texts are authentic. The Protocol will come into force on the signature by Germany of the Instrument of Unconditional Surrender.

The above text of the Protocol between the Governments of the United States of America, the United Kingdom and the Union of Soviet Socialist Republics, on the zones of occupation in Germany and the administration of "Greater Berlin" has been prepared and unanimously adopted by the European Advisory Commission at a meeting held on 12th September, 1944, with the exception of the allocation of the North-Western and South-Western zones of occupation in Germany and the North-Western and Southern parts of "Greater Berlin", which requires further consideration and joint agreement by the Governments of the U.S.A., U.K. and U.S.S.R.

Representative of the Government of the U.S.A. on the European Advisory Commission:

J. G. Winant

JOHN G. WINANT

LANCASTER HOUSE, LONDON, S.W. 1.

Representative of the Government of the U.K. on the European Advisory Commission:

W. Strang

WILLIAM STRANG

LANCASTER HOUSE, LONDON, S.W. 1.

Representative of the Government of the U.S.S.R on the European Advisory Commission:

F. T. Gousev

F. T. GOUSEV

LANCASTER HOUSE, LONDON, S.W. 1.

Document A2

Agreement Amending the Protocol on Zones of Occupation in Germany and Administration of the "Greater Berlin" Area, Approved by the European Advisory Commission, November 14, 1944 [1]

i. In place of the description of the North-Western Zone given in paragraph 2 of the above-mentioned Protocol, the description of the North-Western Zone will read as follows:—

"North-Western Zone (as shown on the annexed map "C" [2]*)*
The territory of Germany situated to the west of the line defined in the description of the Eastern zone, and bounded on the south by a line drawn from the point where the frontier between the Prussian provinces of Hanover and Hessen-Nassau meets the western frontier of the Prussian province of Saxony; thence along the southern frontier of Hanover; thence along the northwestern, western and southern frontiers of Hessen-Nassau to the point where the River Rhine leaves the latter; thence along the center of the navigable channel of the River Rhine to the point where it leaves Hessen-Darmstadt; thence along the western frontier of Baden to the point where this frontier becomes the Franco-German frontier will be occupied by armed forces of the United Kingdom."

2. In place of the description of the South-Western Zone given in paragraph 2 of the above-mentioned Protocol, the description of the South-Western Zone will read as follows:—

"South-Western Zone (as shown on the annexed map "C")
The territory of Germany situated to the south of a line commencing at the junction of the frontiers of Saxony, Bavaria, and Czechoslovakia and extending westward along the northern frontier of Bavaria to the junction of the frontiers of Hessen-Nassau, Thuringia and Bavaria; thence north, west and south along the eastern, northern, western and southern frontiers of Hessen-Nassau to the point where the River Rhine leaves the southern frontier of Hessen-Nassau; thence southwards along the center of the navigable channel of the River Rhine to the point where it leaves Hessen-Darmstadt; thence along the western frontier of Baden to the point where this frontier becomes the Franco-German frontier will be occupied by armed forces of the United States of America."

3. The following additional paragraph will be inserted after the description of the South-Western Zone:—

---

[1] Treaties and Other International Acts Series 3071. This agreement, which amended the protocol of September 12, 1944 (*ante*), was approved by the United Kingdom on December 5, 1944; the United States, February 2, 1945; and the Soviet Union, February 6, 1945. In accordance with the Yalta Agreement (*post*) the protocol was further amended on July 26, 1945, to provide for French occupation zones, both in Germany, and in Greater Berlin (*post*).

[2] Not printed here; see 5 UST 2087.

"For the purpose of facilitating communications between the South-Western Zone and the sea, the Commander-in-Chief of the United States forces in the South-Western Zone will

(a) exercise such control of the ports of Bremen and Bremerhaven and the necessary staging areas in the vicinity thereof as may be agreed hereafter by the United Kingdom and United States military authorities to be necessary to meet his requirements;

(b) enjoy such transit facilities through the North-Western Zone as may be agreed hereafter by the United Kingdom and United States military authorities to be necessary to meet his requirements."

4. At the end of the description of the North-Western part of "Greater Berlin" given in paragraph 2 of the above-mentioned Protocol, insert the following words:—

"the United Kingdom"

5. At the end of the description of the Southern part of "Greater Berlin" given in paragraph 2 of the above-mentioned Protocol, insert the following words:—

"the United States of America"

6. In the English text of the sub-paragraph in paragraph 2 of the above-mentioned Protocol beginning with the words "The frontiers of States (Länder) and Provinces," the words "descriptions to the zones" will read "descriptions of the zones."

The above text of the Agreement regarding Amendments to the Protocol of 12th September, 1944, between the Governments of the United States of America, the United Kingdom and the Union of Soviet Socialist Republics on the zones of occupation in Germany and the administration of "Greater Berlin" has been prepared and unanimously adopted by the European Advisory Commission at a meeting held on the 14th November, 1944.

Document A3

Agreement Further Amending the Protocol of September 12, 1944 To Include France in the Occupation of Germany and Administration of "Greater Berlin", Approved by the European Advisory Commission, July 26, 1945 [1]

The Governments of the United States of America, the Union of Soviet Socialist Republics and the United Kingdom having, pursu-

---

[1] Treaties and Other International Acts Series 3071. This agreement was approved by the United States on July 29, 1945; the United Kingdom, August 2, 1945; France, August 7, 1945; and the Soviet Union, August 13, 1945. See also protocol of September 12, 1944 (*ante*) and amendment of November 14, 1944 (*ante*).

ant to the decision of the Crimea Conference announced on 12th February, 1945, invited the Provisional Government of the French Republic to take part in the occupation of Germany,

The Governments of the United States of America, the Union of Soviet Socialist Republics and the United Kingdom and the Provisional Government of the French Republic have agreed to amend and to supplement the Protocol of 12th September, 1944, between the Governments of the United States of America, the Union of Soviet Socialist Republics and the United Kingdom on the zones of occupation in Germany and the administration of "Greater Berlin", and have reached the following agreement:

1. In the Preamble of the Protocol of 12th September, 1944, add the words "and the Provisional Government of the French Republic" in the enumeration of the participating Governments.

2. In Article 1 of the above-mentioned Protocol, substitute "four" for "three" in the words "three zones", "three Powers" and "three Powers".

3. In the first paragraph of Article 2 of the above-mentioned Protocol, add "and the French Republic" in the enumeration of the participating Powers; substitute "four" for "three" in the words "three zones" and "three zones".

4. In place of the description of the North-Western Zone given in Article 2 of the above-mentioned Protocol, the description of the North-Western Zone will read as follows;

"North-Western (United Kingdom) Zone (as shown on the annexed map "D" [2]*)*

The territory of Germany situated to west of the line defined in the description of the Eastern (Soviet) Zone, and bounded on the south by a line drawn from the point where the frontier between the Prussian provinces of Hanover and Hessen-Nassau meets the western frontier of the Prussian province of Saxony; thence along the southern frontier of Hanover, thence along the south-eastern and south-western frontiers of the Prussian province of Westphalia and along the southern frontiers of the Prussian Regierungsbezirke of Köln and Aachen to the point where this frontier meets the Belgian-German frontier will be occupied by armed forces of the United Kingdom."

5. In place of the descripton of the South-Western Zone given in Article 2 of the above-mentioned Protocol, description of the South-Western Zone will read as follows:—

"South-Western (United States) Zone (as shown on the annexed map "D")

The territory of Germany situated to the south and east of a line commencing at the junction of the frontiers of Saxony, Bavaria and Czechoslovakia and extending westward along the northern frontier of Bavaria to the junction of the fron-

[2] Not printed here; see 5 UST 2093.

32

tiers of Hessen-Nassau, Thuringia and Bavaria; thence north and west along the eastern and northern frontiers of Hessen-Nassau to the point where the frontier of the district of Dill meets the frontier of the district of Oberwesterwald; thence along the western frontier of the district of Dill, the north-western frontier of the district of Oberlahn, the northern and western frontiers of the district of Limburg-Lahn, the north-western frontier of the district of Untertaunus and the northern frontier of the district of Rheingau; thence south and east along the western and southern frontiers of Hessen-Nassau to the point where the River Rhine leaves the southern frontier of Hessen-Nassau; thence southwards along the centre of the navigable channel of the River Rhine to the point where the latter leaves Hessen-Darmstadt; thence along the western frontier of Baden to the point where the frontier of the district of Karlsruhe meets the frontier of the district of Rastatt; thence southeast along the southern frontier of the district of Karlsruhe; thence north-east and south-east along the eastern frontier of Baden to the point where the frontier of Baden meets the frontier between the districts of Calw and Leonberg; thence south and east along the western frontier of the district of Leonberg, the western and southern frontiers of the district of Böblingen, the southern frontier of the district of Nürtingen and the southern frontier of the district of Göppingen to the point where the latter meets the Reichsautobahn between Stuttgart and Ulm; thence along the southern boundary of the Reichsautobahn to the point where the latter meets the western frontier of the district of Ulm; thence south along the western frontier of the district of Ulm to the point where the latter meets the western frontier of the State of Bavaria; thence south along the western frontier of Bavaria to the point where the frontier of the district of Kempten meets the frontier of the district of Lindau; thence south-west along the western frontier of the district of Kempten and the western frontier of the district of Sonthofen to the point where the latter meets the Austro-German frontier will be occupied by armed forces of the United States of America."

6. The following additional paragraph will be inserted in Article 2 of the above-mentioned Protocol, following the description of the South-Western Zone:—

"*Western (French) Zone (as shown on the annexed map "D")*
"The territory of Germany, situated to the south and east of a line commencing at the junction of the frontiers of Belgium and of the Prussian Regierungsbezirke of Trier and Aachen and extending eastward along the northern frontier of the Prussian Regierungsbezirk of Trier; thence north, east and south along the western, northern and eastern frontier of the Prussian Regierungsbezirk of Koblenz to the point where the frontier of Koblenz meets the frontier of the district of Oberwesterwald; thence east, south and west along the northern, eastern and southern frontiers of the district of

Oberwesterwald and along the eastern frontiers of the districts of Unterwesterwald, Unterlahn and Sankt Goarshausen to the point where the frontier of the district of Sankt Goarshausen meets the frontier of the Regierungsbezirk of Koblenz; thence south and east along the eastern frontier of Koblenz; and the northern frontier of Hessen-Darmstadt to the point where the River Rhine leaves the southern frontier of Hessen-Nassau; thence southwards along the centre of the navigable channel of the River Rhine to the point where the latter leaves Hessen-Darmstadt; thence along the western frontier of Baden to the point where the frontier of the district of Karlsruhe meets the frontier of the district of Rastatt; thence south-east along the northern frontier of the district of Rastatt; thence north, east and south along the western, northern and eastern frontiers of the district of Calw; thence eastwards along the northern frontiers of the districts of Horb, Tübingen, Reutlingen and Münsingen to the point where the northern frontier of the district of Münsingen meets the Reichsautobahn between Stuttgart and Ulm; thence southeast along the southern boundary of the Reichsautobahn to the point where the latter meets the eastern frontier of the district of Münsingen; thence south-east along the north-eastern frontiers of the districts of Münsingen, Ehingen and Biberach; thence southwards along the eastern frontiers of the districts of Biberach, Wagen and Lindau to the point where the eastern frontier of the district of Lindau meets the Austro-German frontier will be occupied by armed forces of the French Republic".

7. In the paragraph of Article 2 of the above-mentioned Protocol which relates to the joint occupation of "Greater Berlin", insert "and the French Republic" in the enumeration of the participating Powers; substitute the word "four" for the words "the following three".

8. In Article 3 of the above-mentioned Protocol, substitute "four" for "three" before the word "zones".

9. In Article 4 of the above-mentioned Protocol, substitute "four" for "three" before the word "Powers".

10. In Article 5 of the above-mentioned Protocol, substitute "four" for "three" before the word "Commandants".

11. In Article 6 of the above-mentioned Protocol, substitute "quadruplicate" for "triplicate"; add "French" in the enumeration of the languages; substitute "The three texts" for the words "Both texts".

The above text of the Agreement between the Governments of the United States of America, the Union of Soviet Socialist Republics and the United Kingdom and the Provisional Government of the French Republic, regarding Amendments to the Protocol of 12th September, 1944, on the zones of occupation in Germany and the administration of "Greater Berlin" has been prepared and unanimously adopted by the European Advisory Commission at a meeting held on 26th July, 1945.

Representative of the Government of the United States of America on the European Advisory Commission:

JOHN G. WINANT

LANCASTER HOUSE, LONDON, S.W. 1.
26th July 1945.

Representative of the Government of the Union of Soviet Socialist Republics on the European Advisory Commision:

G. SAKSIN

LANCASTER HOUSE, LONDON, S.W. 1.
26th July 1945.

Representative of the Government of the United Kingdom on the European Commission:

RONALD I. CAMPBELL

LANCASTER HOUSE, LONDON, S.W. 1.
26th July 1945.

Representative of the Provisional Government of the French Republic on the European Advisory Commission:

R. MASSIGLI

LANCASTER HOUSE, LONDON, S.W. 1.
26th July 1945.

Document A4

Agreement on Control Machinery in Germany, Adopted by the European Advisory Commission, November 14, 1944 [1]

The Governments of the United States of America, the United Kingdom of Great Britain and Northern Ireland and the Union of Soviet Socialist Republics have reached the following Agreement with regard to the organisation of the Allied control machinery in Germany in the period during which Germany will be carrying out the basic requirements of unconditional surrender:—

ARTICLE 1.

Supreme authority in Germany will be exercised, on instructions from their respective Governments, by the Commanders-in-Chief of the armed forces of the United States of America, the United Kingdom and the Union of Soviet Socialist Republics, each in his own zone of occupation, and also jointly, in matters affecting Germany as a whole, in their capacity as members of the supreme organ of control constituted under the present Agreement.

ARTICLE 2.

Each Commander-in-Chief in his zone of occupation will have attached to him military, naval and air representatives of the other two Commanders-in-Chief for liaison duties.

---

[1] Treaties and Other International Acts Series 3070. Approved by the United States on January 24, 1945; the Soviet Union, February 6, 1945; and the United Kingdom, December 5, 1944.

ARTICLE 3.

(a) The three Commanders-in-Chief, acting together as a body, will constitute a supreme organ of control called the Control Council.

(b) The functions of the Control Council will be:—

(i) to ensure appropriate uniformity of action by the Commanders-in-Chief in their respective zones of occupation:

(ii) to initiate plans and reach agreed decisions on the chief military, political, economic and other questions affecting Germany as a whole, on the basis of instructions received by each Commander-in-Chief from his Government;

(iii) to control the German central administration, which will operate under the direction of the Control Council and will be responsible to it for ensuring compliance with its demands;

(iv) to direct the administration of "Greater Berlin" through appropriate organs.

(c) The Control Council will meet at least once in ten days; and it will meet at any time upon request of any one of its members. Decisions of the Control Council shall be unanimous. The chairmanship of the Control Council will be held in rotation by each of its three members.

(d) Each member of the Control Council will be assisted by a political adviser, who will, when necessary, attend meetings of the Control Council. Each member of the Control Council may also, when necessary, be assisted at meetings of the Council by naval or air advisers.

ARTICLE 4.

A permanent Co-ordinating Committee will be established under the Control Council, composed of one representative of each of the three Commanders-in-Chief, not below the rank of General Officer or the equivalent rank in the naval or air forces. Members of the Co-ordinating Committee will, when necessary, attend meetings of the Control Council.

ARTICLE 5.

The duties of the Co-ordinating Committee, acting on behalf of the Control Council and through the Control Staff, will include:—

(a) the carrying out of the decisions of the Control Council;

(b) the day-to-day supervision and control of the activities of the German central administration and institutions;

(c) the co-ordination of current problems which call for uniform measures in all three zones;

(d) the preliminary examination and preparation for the Control Council of all questions submitted by individual Commanders-in-Chief.

ARTICLE 6.

(a) The members of the Control Staff appointed by their respective national authorities, will be organized in the following Divisions:—

Military; Naval; Air; Transport; Political; Economic; Finance; Reparations, Deliveries and Restitution; Internal Affairs and Communications; Legal; Prisoners of War and Displaced Persons; Man-power.

Adjustments in the number and functions of the Divisions may be made in the light of experience.

(b) At the head of each Division there will be three high-ranking officials, one from each Power. The duties of the three heads of each Division, acting jointly, will include:—

(i) exercising control over the corresponding German Ministries and German central institutions;

(ii) acting as advisers to the Control Council and, when necessary, attending meetings thereof;

(iii) transmitting to the German central administration the decisions of the Control Council, communicated through the Co-ordinating Committee.

(c) The three heads of a Division will take part in meetings of the Co-ordinating Committee at which matters affecting the work of their Division are on the agenda.

(d) The staffs of the Divisions may include civilian as well as military personnel. They may also, in special cases, include nationals of other United Nations, appointed in their personal capacity.

ARTICLE 7.

(a) An Inter-Allied Governing Authority (Komandatura) consisting of three Commandants, one from each Power, appointed by their respective Commanders-in-Chief, will be established to direct jointly the administration of the "Greater Berlin" area. Each of the Commandants will serve in rotation, in the position of Chief Commandant, as head of the Inter-Allied Governing Authority.

(b) A Technical Staff, consisting of personnel of each of the three Powers, will be established under the Inter-Allied Governing Authority, and will be organised to serve the purpose of supervising and controlling the activities of the local organs of "Greater Berlin" which are responsible for its municipal services.

(c) The Inter-Allied Governing Authority will operate under the general direction of the Control Council and will receive orders through the Co-ordinating Committee.

ARTICLE 8.

The necessary liaison with the Governments of other United Nations chiefly interested will be ensured by the appointment of such Governments of military missions (which may include civilian members) to the Control Council, having access, through the appropriate channels, to the organs of control.

ARTICLE 9.

United Nations' organisations which may be admitted by the Control Council to operate in Germany will, in respect to their activities in Germany, be subordinate to the Allied control machinery and answerable to it.

ARTICLE 10.

The Allied organs for the control and administration of Germany outlined above will operate during the initial period of the occupation of Germany immediately following surrender, that is, the period when Germany is carrying out the basic requirements of unconditional surrender.

ARTICLE 11.

The question of the Allied organs required for carrying out the functions of control and administration in Germany in a later period will be the subject of a separate Agreement between the Governments of the United States of America, the United Kingdom and the Union of Soviet Socialist Republics.

The above text of the Agreement on Control Machinery in Germany between the Governments of the United States of America, the United Kingdom and the Union of Soviet Socialist Republics has been prepared and unanimously adopted by the Representatives of the United States of America, the United Kingdom and the Union of Soviet Socialist Republics on the European Advisory Commission at a meeting held on 14th November, 1944, and is now submitted to their respective Governments for approval.

For the Representative of the Government of the United States of America on the European Advisory Commission:

PHILIP E. MOSELY

LANCASTER HOUSE, LONDON, S.W. 1.
14th November, 1944.

Representative of the Government of the United Kingdom on the European Advisory Commission;

WILLIAM STRANG

LANCASTER HOUSE, LONDON, S.W. 1.
14th November, 1944.

Representative of the Government of the Union of Soviet Socialist Republics on the European Advisory Commission:

F T GOUSEV

LANCASTER HOUSE, LONDON, S.W. 1.
14th November, 1944.

Document A5

Declaration Regarding the Defeat of Germany and the Assumption of Supreme Authority by the Allied Powers, Signed at Berlin, June 5, 1945 [1]

The German Armed Forces on land, at sea and in the air have been completely defeated and have surrendered unconditionally and Germany, which bears responsibility for the war, is no longer capable of resisting the will of the victorious Powers. The unconditional surrender of Germany has thereby been effected, and Germany has become subject to such requirements as may now or hereafter be imposed upon her.

There is no central Government or authority in Germany capable of accepting responsibility for the maintenance of order, the administration of the country and compliance with the requirements of the victorious Powers.

It is in these circumstances necessary, without prejudice to any subsequent decisions that may be taken respecting Germany, to make provision for the cessation of any further hostilities on the part of the German armed forces, for the maintenance of order in Germany and for the administration of the country, and to announce the immediate requirements with which Germany must comply.

The Representatives of the Supreme Commands of the United States of America, the Union of Soviet Socialist Republics, the United Kingdom and the French Republic, hereinafter called the "Allied Representatives," acting by authority of their respective Governments and the interests of the United Nations, accordingly make the following Declaration:—

The Governments of the United States of America, the Union of Soviet Socialist Republics and the United Kingdom, and the Provisional Government of the French Republic, hereby assume supreme authority with respect to Germany, including all the powers possessed by the German Government, the High Command and any state, municipal, or local government or authority. The assumption, for the purposes stated above, of the said authority and powers does not affect the annexation of Germany.

The Governments of the United States of America, the Union of Soviet Socialist Republics and the United Kingdom, and the Provisional Government of the French Republic, will hereafter determine the boundaries of Germany or any part thereof and the status of Germany or of any area at present being part of German territory.

In virtue of the supreme authority and powers thus assumed by the four Governments, the Allied Representatives announce the following requirements arising from the complete defeat and unconditional surrender of Germany with which Germans must comply:—

ARTICLE 1.

Germany, and all German military, naval and air authorities and all forces under German control shall immediately cease hostilities in all theatres of war against the forces of the United Nations on land, at sea and in the air.

ARTICLE 2.

(a) All armed forces of Germany or under German control, wherever they may be situated, including land, air, anti-aircraft and naval forces, the S.S., S.A. and Gestapo, and all other forces of auxiliary organizations equipped with weapons, shall be completely disarmed, handing over their weapons and equipment to local Allied Commanders or to officers designated by the Allied Representatives.

(b) The personnel of the formations and units of all the forces referred to in paragraph (a) above shall, at the discretion of the Commander-in-Chief of the Armed Forces of the Allied State concerned, be declared to be prisoners of war, pending further decisions, and shall be subject to such conditions and directions as may be prescribed by the respective Allied Representatives.

(c) All forces referred to in paragraph (a) above, wherever they may be, will remain in their present positions pending instructions from the Allied Representatives.

(d) Evacuation by the said forces of all territories outside the frontiers of Germany as they existed on the 31st December, 1937, will proceed according to instructions to be given by the Allied Representatives.

(e) Detachments of civil police to be armed with small arms only, for the maintenance of order and for guard duties, will be designated by the Allied Representatives.

ARTICLE 3.

(a) All aircraft of any kind or nationality in Germany or German-occupied or controlled territories or waters, military, naval or civil, other than aircraft in the service of the Allies, will remain on the ground, on the water or aboard ships pending further instructions.

(b) All German or German-controlled aircraft in or over territories or waters not occupied or controlled by Germany will proceed to Germany or to such other place or places as may be specified by the Allied Representatives.

ARTICLE 4.

(a) All German or German-controlled naval vessels, surface and submarine, auxiliary naval craft, and merchant and other shipping wherever such vessels may be at the time of this Declaration, and all other merchant ships of whatever nationality in German ports, will remain in or proceed immediately to ports and bases as specified by the Allied Representatives. The crews of such vessels will remain on board pending further instructions.

(b) All ships and vessels of the United Nations, whether or not title has been transferred as the result of prize court or other proceedings, which are at the disposal of Germany or under German control at the time of this Declaration, will proceed at the dates and to the ports and bases specified by the Allied Representatives.

ARTICLE 5.

(a) All or any of the following articles in the possession of the German armed forces or under German control or at German disposal will be held intact and in good condition at the disposal of the Allied Representatives, for such purposes and at such times and places as they may prescribe:—

(i) all arms, ammunition, explosives, military equipment, stores and supplies and other implements of war of all kinds and all other war materials;

(ii) all naval vessels of all classes, both surface and submarine auxiliary naval craft and all merchant shipping, whether afloat, under repair or construction, built or building;

(iii) all aircraft of all kinds, aviation and antiaircraft equipment and devices;

(iv) all transportation and communications facilities and equipment, by land, water or air;

(v) all military installations and establishments, including airfields, seaplane bases, ports and naval bases, storage depots, permanent and temporary land and coast fortifications, fortresses and other fortified areas, together with plans and drawings of all such fortifications, installations and establishments;

(vi) all factories, plants, shops, research institutions, laboratories, testing stations, technical data, patents, plans, drawings and inventions, designed or intended to produce or to facilitate the production or use of the articles, materials, and facilities referred to in sub-paragraphs (i), (ii), (iii), (iv) and (v) above or otherwise to further the conduct of war.

(b) At the demand of the Allied Representatives the following will be furnished:—

(i) the labour, services and plant required for the maintenance or for operation of any of the six categories mentioned in paragraph (a) above; and

(ii) any information or records that may be required by the Allied Representatives in connection with the same.

(c) At the demand of the Allied Representatives all facilities will be provided for the movement of Allied troops and agencies, their equipment and supplies, on the railways, roads and other land communications or by sea, river or air. All means of transportation will be maintained in good order and repair, and the labour, services and plant necessary therefor will be furnished.

ARTICLE 6.

(a) The German authorities will release to the Allied Representatives, in accordance with the procedure to be laid down by them, all prisoners of war at present in their power, belonging to the forces of the United Nations, and will furnish full lists of these persons, indicating the places of their detention in Germany or territory occupied by Germany. Pending the release of such prisoners of war, the German authorities and people will protect them in their persons and property and provide them with adequate food, clothing, shelter, medical attention and money in accordance with their rank or official position.

(b) The German authorities and people will in like manner provide for and release all other nationals of the United Nations who are confined, interned or otherwise under restraint, and all other persons who may be confined, interned or otherwise under restraint for political reasons or as a result of any Nazi action, law or regulation which discriminates on the ground of race, colour, creed or political belief.

(c) The German authorities will, at the demand of the Allied Representatives, hand over control of places of detention to such officers as may be designated for the purpose by the Allied Representatives.

ARTICLE 7.

The German authorities concerned will furnish to the Allied Representatives:—

(a) full information regarding the forces referred to in Article 2(a), and, in particular, will furnish forthwith all information which the Allied Representatives may require concerning the numbers, locations and dispositions of such forces, whether located inside or outside of Germany;

(b) complete and detailed information concerning mines, minefields and other obstacles to movement by land, sea or air, and the safety lanes in connection therewith. All such safety lanes will be kept open and clearly marked; all mines, minefields and other dangerous obstacles will as far as possible be rendered safe, and all aids to navigation will be reinstated. Unarmed German military and civilian personnel with the necessary equipment will be made available and utilised for the above purposes and for the removal of mines, minefields and other obstacles as directed by the Allied Representatives.

ARTICLE 8.

There shall be no destruction, removal, concealment, transfer or scuttling of, or damage to, any military, naval, air, shipping, port, industrial and other like property and facilities and all records and archives, wherever they may be situated, except as may be directed by the Allied Representatives.

ARTICLE 9.

Pending the institution of control by the Allied Representatives over all means of communication, all radio and telecommunications installations and other forms of wire or wireless communications, whether ashore or afloat, under German control, will cease transmission except as directed by the Allied Representatives.

ARTICLE 10.

The forces, ships, aircraft, military equipment and other property in Germany or in German control or service or at German disposal, of any other country at war with any of the Allies, will be subject to the provisions of this Declaration and of any proclamations, orders, ordinances or instructions issued thereunder.

ARTICLE 11.

(a) The principal Nazi leaders as specified by the Allied Representatives, and all persons from time to time named or designated by rank, office or employment by the Allied Representatives as being suspected of having committed, ordered or abetted war crimes or analogous offences, will be apprehended and surrendered to the Allied Representatives.

(b) The same will apply in the case of any national of any of the United Nations who is alleged to have committed an offence against his national law, and who may at any time be named or designated by rank, office or employment by the Allied Representatives.

(c) The German authorities and people will comply with any instructions given by the Allied Representatives for the apprehension and surrender of such persons.

ARTICLE 12.

The Allied Representatives will station forces and civil agencies in any or all parts of Germany as they may determine.

ARTICLE 13.

(a) In the exercise of the supreme authority with respect to Germany assumed by the Governments of the United States of America, the Union of Soviet Socialist Republics and the United Kingdom, and the Provisional Government of the French Republic, the four Allied Governments will take such steps, including the complete disarmament and demilitarisation of Germany, as they deem requisite for future peace and security.

(b) The Allied Representatives will impose on Germany additional political, administrative, economic, financial, military and other requirements arising from the complete defeat of Germany. The Allied Representatives, or persons or agencies duly designated to act on their authority, will issue proclamations, orders, ordinances and instructions for the purpose of laying down such additional requirements, and of giving effect to the other provisions of this Declaration. All German authorities and the German people shall carry out unconditionally the requirements of the Allied Representatives, and shall fully comply with all such proclamations, orders, ordinances and instructions.

ARTICLE 14.

This Declaration enters into force and effect at the date and hour set forth below. In the event of failure on the part of the German authorities or people promptly and completely to fulfil their obligations hereby or hereafter imposed, the Allied Representatives will take whatever action may be deemed by them to be appropriate under the circumstances.

ARTICLE 15.

This Declaration is drawn up in the English, Russian, French, and German languages. The English, Russian and French are the only authentic texts.

BERLIN, GERMANY,
June 5, 1945 [2]

---

[2] Signed at 1800 hours, Berlin time, by Dwight D. Eisenhower, General of the Army, USA; Zhukov, Marshal of the Soviet Union; B. L. Montgomery, Field Marshal, Great Britain; De Lattre de Tassigny, General d'Armée, French Provisional Government. [Footnote in the source text.]

Document A6

Protocol of the Proceedings of the Berlin (Potsdam) Conference, August 1, 1945 [1]

[Extracts]

The Berlin Conference of the Three Heads of Government of the U.S.S.R., U.S.A., and U.K., which took place from July 17 to August 2, 1945, came to the following conclusions:

I. ESTABLISHMENT OF A COUNCIL OF FOREIGN MINISTERS

A. The Conference reached the following agreement for the establishment of a Council of Foreign Ministers to do the necessary preparatory work for the peace settlements:

"(1) There shall be established a Council composed of the Foreign Ministers of the United Kingdom, the Union of Soviet Socialist Republics, China, France, and the United States.

"(2) (i) The Council shall normally meet in London which shall be the permanent seat of the joint Secretariat which the Council will form. Each of the Foreign Ministers will be accompanied by a high-ranking Deputy, duly authorized to carry on the work of the Council in the absence of his Foreign Minister, and by a small staff of technical advisers.

"(ii) The first meeting of the Council shall be held in London not later than September 1st 1945. Meetings may be held by common agreement in other capitals as may be agreed from time to time.

"(3) (i) As its immediate important task, the Council shall be authorized to draw up, with a view to their submission to the United Nations, treaties of peace with Italy, Rumania, Bulgar-

---

[1] Department of State press release 238, March 24, 1947. For the detailed record, see *Foreign Relations*, The Conference of Berlin (The Potsdam Conference), 1945.

ia, Hungary and Finland, and to propose settlements of territorial questions outstanding on the termination of the war in Europe. The Council shall be utilized for the preparation of a peace settlement for Germany to be accepted by the Government of Germany when a government adequate for the purpose is established.

"(ii) For the discharge of each of these tasks the Council will be composed of the Members representing those States which were signatory to the terms of surrender imposed upon the enemy State concerned. For the purposes of the peace settlement for Italy, France shall be regarded as a signatory to the terms of surrender for Italy. Other Members will be invited to participate when matters directly concerning them are under discussion.

"(iii) Other matters may from time to time be referred to the Council by agreement between the Member Governments.

"(4) (i) Whenever the Council is considering a question of direct interest to a State not represented thereon, such State should be invited to send representatives to participate in the discussion and study of that question.

"(ii) The Council may adapt its procedure to the particular problems under consideration. In some cases it may hold its own preliminary discussions prior to the participation of other interested States. In other cases, the Council may convoke a formal conference of the State[s] chiefly interested in seeking a solution of the particular problem."

B. It was agreed that the three Governments should each address an identical invitation to the Governments of China and France to adopt this text and to join in establishing the Council. The text of the approved invitation was as follows:

.   .   .   .

C. It was understood that the establishment of the Council of Foreign Ministers for the specific purposes named in the text would be without prejudice to the agreement of the Crimea Conference that there should be periodical consultation between the Foreign Secretaries of the United States, the Union of Soviet Socialist Republics and the United Kingdom.

D. The Conference also considered the position of the European Advisory Commission in the light of the Agreement to establish the Council of Foreign Ministers. It was noted with satisfaction that the Commission had ably discharged its principal tasks by the recommendations that it had furnished for the terms of surrender for Germany, for the zones of occupation in Germany and Austria and for the Inter-Allied control machinery in those countries. It was felt that further work of a detailed character for the coordination of Allied policy for the control of Germany and Austria would in future fall within the competence of the Control Council at Berlin and the Allied Commission at Vienna. Accordingly it was agreed to recommend that the European Advisory Commission be dissolved.

PAUL B. STARES

II. The Principles To Govern the Treatment of Germany in the Initial Control Period

A. POLITICAL PRINCIPLES

1. In accordance with the Agreement on Control Machinery in Germany, supreme authority in Germany is exercised, on instructions from their respective Governments, by the Commanders-in-Chief of the armed forces of the United States of America, the United Kingdom, the Union of Soviet Socialist Republics, and the French Republic, each in his own zone of occupation, and also jointly, in matters affecting Germany as a whole, in their capacity as members of the Control Council.

2. So far as is practicable, there shall be uniformity of treatment of the German population throughout Germany.

3. The purposes of the occupation of Germany by which the Control Council shall be guided are:

(i) The complete disarmament and demilitarization of Germany and the elimination or control of all German industry that could be used for military production. To these ends:

(a) All German land, naval and air forces, the S.S., S.A., S.D., and Gestapo, with all their organizations, staffs and institutions, including the General Staff, the Officers' Corps, Reserve Corps, military schools, war veterans' organizations and all other military and semi-military organizations, together with all clubs and associations which serve to keep alive the military tradition in Germany, shall be completely and finally abolished in such manner as permanently to prevent the revival or reorganization of German militarism and Nazism;

(b) All arms, ammunition and implements of war and all specialized facilities for their production shall be held at the disposal of the Allies or destroyed. The maintenance and production of all aircraft and all arms, ammunition and implements of war shall be prevented.

(ii) To convince the German people that they have suffered a total military defeat and that they cannot escape responsibility for what they have brought upon themselves, since their own ruthless warfare and the fanatical Nazi resistance have destroyed Germany economy and made chaos and suffering inevitable.

(iii) To destroy the National Socialist Party and its affiliated and supervised organizations, to dissolve all Nazi institutions, to ensure that they are not revived in any form, and to prevent all Nazi and militarist activity or propaganda.

(iv) To prepare for the eventual reconstruction of German political life on a democratic basis and for eventual peaceful cooperation in international life by Germany.

4. All Nazi laws which provided the basis of the Hitler regime or established discriminations on grounds of race, creed, or political

48

opinion shall be abolished. No such discriminations, whether legal, administrative or otherwise, shall be tolerated.

5. War criminals and those who have participated in planning or carrying out Nazi enterprises involving or resulting in atrocities or war crimes shall be arrested and brought to judgment. Nazi leaders, influential Nazi supporters and high officials of Nazi organizations and institutions and any other persons dangerous to the occupation or its objectives shall be arrested and interned.

6. All members of the Nazi Party who have been more than nominal participants in its activities and all other persons hostile to Allied purposes shall be removed from public and semi-public office, and from positions of responsibility in important private undertakings. Such persons shall be replaced by persons who, by their political and moral qualities, are deemed capable of assisting in developing genuine democratic institutions in Germany.

7. German education shall be so controlled as completely to eliminate Nazi and militarist doctrines and to make possible the successful development of democratic ideas.

8. The judicial system will be reorganized in accordance with the principles of democracy, of justice under law, and of equal rights for all citizens without distinction of race, nationality or religion.

9. The administration in Germany should be directed towards the decentralization of the political structure and the development of local responsibility. To this end:

> (i) local self-government shall be restored throughout Germany on democratic principles and in particular through elective councils as rapidly as is consistent with military security and the purposes of military occupation;
> (ii) all democratic political parties with rights of assembly and of public discussion shall be allowed and encouraged throughout Germany;
> (iii) representative and elective principles shall be introduced into regional, provincial and state (land) administration as rapidly as may be justified by the successful application of these principles in local self-government;
> (iv) for the time being, no central German Government shall be established. Notwithstanding this, however, certain essential central German administrative departments, headed by State Secretaries, shall be established, particularly in the fields of finance, transport, communications, foreign trade and industry. Such departments will act under the direction of the Control Council.

10. Subject to the necessity for maintaining military security, freedom of speech, press and religion shall be permitted, and religious institutions shall be respected. Subject likewise to the maintenance of military security, the formation of free trade unions shall be permitted.

B. ECONOMIC PRINCIPLES

11. In order to eliminate Germany's war potential, the production of arms, ammunition and implements of war as well as all

types of aircraft and sea-going ships shall be prohibited and prevented. Production of metals, chemicals, machinery and other items that are directly necessary to a war economy shall be rigidly controlled and restricted to Germany's approved post-war peacetime needs to meet the objectives stated in Paragraph 15. Productive capacity not needed for permitted production shall be removed in accordance with the reparations plan recommended by the Allied Commission on Reparations and approved by the Governments concerned or if not removed shall be destroyed.

12. At the earliest practicable date, the German economy shall be decentralized for the purpose of eliminating the present excessive concentration of economic power as exemplified in particular by cartels, syndicates, trusts and other monopolistic arrangements.

13. In organizing the German economy, primary emphasis shall be given to the development of agriculture and peaceful domestic industries.

14. During the period of occupation Germany shall be treated as a single economic unit. To this end common policies shall be established in regard to:

(a) mining and industrial production and its allocation;
(b) agriculture, forestry and fishing;
(c) wages, prices and rationing;
(d) import and export programs for Germany as a whole;
(e) currency and banking, central taxation and customs;
(f) reparation and removal of industrial war potential;
(g) transportation and communications.

In applying these policies account shall be taken, where appropriate, of varying local conditions.

15. Allied controls shall be imposed upon the German economy but only to the extent necessary:

(a) to carry out programs of industrial disarmament, demilitarization, or reparations, and of approved exports and imports.

(b) to assure the production and maintenance of goods and services required to meet the needs of the occupying forces and displaced persons in Germany and essential to maintain in Germany average living standards not exceeding the average of the standards of living of European countries. (European countries means all European countries excluding the United Kingdom and the U.S.S.R.)

(c) to ensure in the manner determined by the Control Council equitable distribution of essential commodities between the several zones so as to produce a balanced economy throughout Germany and reduce the need for imports.

(d) to control German industry and all economic and financial international transactions including exports and imports, with the aim of preventing Germany from developing a war potential and of achieving the other objectives named herein.

(e) to control all German public or private scientific bodies, research and experimental institutions, laboratories, et cetera, connected with economic activities.

16. In the imposition and maintenance of economic controls established by the Control Council, German administrative machinery shall be created and the German authorities shall be required to the fullest extent practicable to proclaim and assume administration of such controls. Thus it should be brought home to the German people that the responsibility for the administration of such controls and any breakdown in these controls will rest with themselves. Any German controls which may run counter to the objectives of occupation will be prohibited.

17. Measures shall be promptly taken:

(a) to effect essential repair of transport;
(b) to enlarge coal production;
(c) to maximize agricultural output; and
(d) to effect emergency repair of housing and essential utilities.

18. Appropriate steps shall be taken by the Control Council to exercise control and the power of disposition over the German-owned external assets not already under the control of United Nations which have taken part in the war against Germany.

19. Payment of Reparations should leave enough resources to enable the German people to subsist without external assistance. In working out the economic balance of Germany the necessary means must be provided to pay for imports approved by the Control Council in Germany. The proceeds of exports from current production and stocks shall be available in the first place for payment for such imports.

The above clause will not apply to the equipment and products referred to in paragraphs 4(a) and 4(b) of the Reparations Agreement.

III. Reparations From Germany

1. Reparations claims of the U.S.S.R. shall be met by removals from the zone of Germany occupied by the U.S.S.R., and from appropriate German external assets.

2. The U.S.S.R. undertakes to settle the reparations claims of Poland from its own share of reparations.

3. The reparation claims of the United States, the United Kingdom and other countries entitled to reparations shall be met from the Western Zones and from appropriate German external assets.

4. In addition to the reparations to be taken by the U.S.S.R. from its own zone of occupation, the U.S.S.R. shall receive additionally from the Western Zones:

(a) 15 percent of such usable and complete industrial capital equipment, in the first place from the metallurgical, chemical and machine manufacturing industries as is unnecessary for the German peace economy and should be removed from the Western Zones of Germany, in exchange for an equivalent value of food, coal, potash, zinc, timber, clay products, petroleum products, and such other commodities as may be agreed upon.

(b) 10 percent of such industrial capital equipment as is unnecessary for the German peace economy and should be removed from the Western Zones, to be transferred to the Soviet Government on reparations account without payment or exchange of any kind in return.

Removals of equipment as provided in (a) and (b) above shall be made simultaneously.

5. The amount of equipment to be removed from the Western Zones on account of reparations must be determined within six months from now at the latest.

6. Removals of industrial capital equipment shall begin as soon as possible and shall be completed within two years from the determination specified in paragraph 5. The delivery of products covered by 4(a) above shall begin as soon as possible and shall be made by the U.S.S.R. in agreed installments within five years of the date hereof. The determination of the amount and character of the industrial capital equipment unnecessary for the German peace economy and therefore available for reparation shall be made by the Control Council under policies fixed by the Allied Commission on Reparations, with the participation of France, subject to the final approval of the Zone Commander in the Zone from which the equipment is to be removed.

7. Prior to the fixing of the total amount of equipment subject to removal, advance deliveries shall be made in respect to such equipment as will be determined to be eligible for delivery in accordance with the procedure set forth in the last sentence of paragraph 6.

8. The Soviet Government renounces all claims in respect of reparations to shares of German enterprises which are located in the Western Zones of Germany as well as to German foreign assets in all countries except those specified in paragraph 9 below.

9. The Governments of the U.K. and U.S.A. renounce all claims in respect of reparations to shares of German enterprises which are located in the Eastern Zone of occupation in Germany, as well as to German foreign assets in Bulgaria, Finland, Hungary, Rumania and Eastern Austria.

10. The Soviet Government makes no claims to gold captured by the Allied troops in Germany.

IV. DISPOSAL OF THE GERMAN NAVY AND MERCHANT MARINE

A. The following principles for the distribution of the German Navy were agreed:

(1) The total strength of the German surface navy, excluding ships sunk and those taken over from Allied Nations, but including ships under construction or repair, shall be divided equally among the U.S.S.R., U.K. and U.S.A.

(2) Ships under construction or repair mean those ships whose construction or repair may be completed within three to six months, according to the type of ship. Whether such ships under construction or repair shall be completed or repaired shall be determined by the technical commission appointed by the Three Powers and referred to below, subject to the principle that their completion or repair must be achieved within

the time limits above provided, without any increase of skilled employment in the German shipyards and without permitting the reopening of any German ship building or connected industries. Completion date means the date when a ship is able to go out on its first trip, or, under peacetime standards, would refer to the customary date of delivery by shipyard to the Government.

(3) The larger part of the German submarine fleet shall be sunk. Not more than thirty submarines shall be preserved and divided equally between the U.S.S.R., U.K. and U.S.A. for experimental and technical purposes.

(4) All stocks of armament, ammunition and supplies of German Navy appertaining to the vessels transferred pursuant to paragraph (1) and (3) hereof shall be handed over to the respective powers receiving such ships.

(5) The Three Governments agree to constitute a tripartite naval commission comprising two representatives for each government, accompanied by the requisite staff, to submit agreed recommendations to the Three Governments for the allocation of specific German warships and to handle other detailed matters arising out of the agreement between the Three Governments regarding the German fleet. The Commission will hold its first meeting not later than 15th August, 1945, in Berlin, which shall be its headquarters. Each Delegation on the Commission will have the right on the basis of reciprocity to inspect German warships wherever they may be located.

(6) The Three Governments agreed that transfers, including those of ships under construction and repair, shall be completed as soon as possible, but not later than 15th February, 1946. The Commission will submit fortnightly reports, including proposals for the progressive allocation of the vessels when agreed by the Commission.

B. The following principles for the distribution of the German Merchant Marine were agreed:

(1) The German Merchant Marine, surrendered to the Three Powers and wherever located, shall be divided equally among the U.S.S.R., the U.K., and the U.S.A. The actual transfers of the ships to the respective countries shall take place as soon as practicable after the end of the war against Japan. The United Kingdom and the United States will provide out of their shares of the surrendered German merchant ships appropriate amounts for other Allied States whose merchant marines have suffered heavy losses in the common cause against Germany, except that the Soviet Union shall provide out of its share for Poland.

(2) The allocation, manning, and operation of these ships during the Japanese War period shall fall under the cognizance and authority of the Combined Shipping Adjustment Board and the United Maritime Authority.

(3) While actual transfer of the ships shall be delayed until after the end of the war with Japan, a Tripartite Shipping Commission shall inventory and value all available ships and

recommend a specific distribution in accordance with paragraph (1).

(4) German inland and coastal ships determined to be necessary to the maintenance of the basic German peace economy by the Allied Control Council of Germany shall not be included in the shipping pool thus divided among the Three Powers.

(5) The Three Governments agree to constitute a tripatrite merchant marine commission comprising two representatives for each Government, accompanied by the requisite staff, to submit agreed recommendations to the Three Governments for the allocation of specific German merchant ships and to handle other detailed matters arising out of the agreement between the Three Governments regarding the German merchant ships. The Commission will hold its first meeting not later than September 1st, 1945, in Berlin, which shall be its headquarters. Each delegation on the Commission will have the right on the basis of reciprocity to inspect the German merchant ships wherever they may be located.

V. City of Koenigsberg and the Adjacent Area

The Conference examined a proposal by the Soviet Government to the effect that pending the final determination of territorial questions at the peace settlement, the section of the western frontier of the Union of Soviet Socialist Republics which is adjacent to the Baltic Sea should pass from a point on the eastern shore of the Bay of Danzig to the east, north of Braunsberg Goldap, to the meeting point of the frontiers of Lithuania, the Polish Republic and East Prussia.

The Conference has agreed in principle to the proposal of the Soviet Government concerning the ultimate transfer to the Soviet Union of the City of Koenigsberg and the area adjacent to it as described above subject to expert examination of the actual frontier.

The President of the United States and the British Prime Minister have declared that they will support the proposal of the Conference at the forthcoming peace settlement.

VI. War Criminals

The Three Governments have taken note of the discussions which have been proceeding in recent weeks in London between British, United States, Soviet and French representatives with a view to reaching agreement on the methods of trial of these major war criminals whose crimes under the Moscow Declaration of October, 1943, have no particular geographical localisation. The three Goverments reaffirm their intention to bring these criminals to swift and sure justice. They hope that the negotiations in London will result in speedy agreement being reached for this purpose, and they regard it as a matter of great importance that the trial of these major criminals should begin at the earliest possible date. The first list of defendants will be published before 1st September.

VIII. Poland

B. WESTERN FRONTIER OF POLAND

In conformity with the agreement on Poland reached at the Crimea Conference the three Heads of Government have sought the opinion of the Polish Provisional Government of National Unity in regard to the accession of territory in the north and west which Poland should receive. The President of the National Council of Poland and members of the Polish Provisional Government of National Unity have been received at the Conference and have fully presented their views. The three Heads of Government reaffirm their opinion that the final delimitation of the western frontier of Poland should await the peace settlement.

The three Heads of Government agree that, pending the final determination of Poland's western frontier, the former German territories east of a line running from the Baltic Sea immediately west of Swinemunde, and thence along the Oder River to the confluence of the western Neisse River and along the western Neisse to the Czechoslovak frontier, including that portion of East Prussia not placed under the administration of the Union of Soviet Socialist Republics in accordance with the understanding reached at this conference and including the area of the former free city of Danzig, shall be under the administration of the Polish State and for such purposes should not be considered as part of the Soviet zone of occupation in Germany.

●　　　●　　　●　　　●　　　●　　　●　　　●

XII. Orderly Transfer of German Populations

The Three Governments, having considered the question in all its aspects, recognize that the transfer to Germany of German populations, or elements thereof, remaining in Poland, Czechoslovakia and Hungary, will have to be undertaken. They agree that any transfers that take place should be effected in an orderly and humane manner.

Since the influx of a large number of Germans into Germany would increase the burden already resting on the occupying authorities, they consider that the Control Council in Germany should in the first instance examine the problem with special regard to the question of the equitable distribution of these Germans among the several zones of occupation. They are accordingly instructing their respective representatives on the Control Council to report to their Governments as soon as possible the extent to which such persons have already entered Germany from Poland, Czechoslovakia and Hungary, and to submit an estimate of the time and rate at which further transfers could be carried out having regard to the present situation in Germany.

The Czechoslovak Government, the Polish Provisional Government and the Control Council in Hungary are at the same time being informed of the above and are being requested meanwhile to suspend further expulsions pending an examination by the Governments concerned of the report from their representatives on the Control Council.

. . . .

XIX. DIRECTIVES TO MILITARY COMMANDERS ON ALLIED CONTROL COUNCIL FOR GERMANY

The Three Governments agreed that each would send a directive to its representative on the Control Council for Germany informing him of all decisions of the Conference affecting matters within the scope of his duties.

. . . .

XX. USE OF ALLIED PROPERTY FOR SATELLITE REPARATIONS OR "WAR TROPHIES"

The proposal (Annex II) presented by the United States Delegation was accepted in principle by the Conference, but the drafting of an agreement on the matter was left to be worked out through diplomatic channels.

. . . .

Annex II

USE OF ALLIED PROPERTY FOR SATELLITE REPARATIONS OR "WAR TROPHIES"

1. The burden of reparations and "war trophies" should not fall on Allied nationals.

2. *Capital Equipment.* We object to the removal of such Allied property as reparations, "war trophies", or under any other guise. Loss would accrue to Allied nationals as a result of destruction of plants and the consequent loss of markets and trading connections. Seizure of Allied property makes impossible the fulfillment by the satellite of its obligation under the armistice to restore intact the rights and interests of the Allied Nations and their nationals.

The United States looks to the other occupying powers for the return of any equipment already removed and the cessation of removals. Where such equipment will not or cannot be returned, the U.S. will demand of the satellite adequate, effective and prompt compensation to American nationals, and that such compensation have priority equal to that of the reparations payment.

These principles apply to all property wholly or substantially owned by Allied nationals. In the event of removals of property in which the American as well as the entire Allied interest is less than substantial, the U.S. expects adequate, effective, and prompt compensation.

3. *Current Production.* While the U.S. does not oppose reparations out of current production of Allied investments, the satellite

must provide immediate and adequate compensation to the Allied nationals including sufficient foreign exchange or products so that they can recover reasonable foreign currency expenditures and transfer a reasonable return on their investment. Such compensation must also have equal priority with reparations.

We deem it essential that the satellites not conclude treaties, agreements or arrangements which deny to Allied nationals access, on equal terms, to their trade, raw materials and industry; and appropriately modify any existing arrangements which may have that effect.

Document A7

Notes of a Conference Among Marshal Zhukov, General Clay, and General Weeks on Surface and Air Access to Berlin, June 29, 1945 [1]

[Extract]

•　　•　　•　　•　　•　　•　　•

Marshal Zhukov stated he received requests for railroads from Berlin to Hamburg and Bremen, Berlin-Stendal-Hannover, Berlin-Brandenburg-Magdeburg-Hannover, and a 2½ kilometer rail line within the Russian zone; that he had requests for two highways, one from Berlin through Dessau, Halle, Erfurt, Eisenach, Kassel to Frankfurt, and the other from Berlin-Magdeburg-Braunschweig; and requests for air lanes from Berlin to Bremen as well as Berlin to Frankfurt. It was apparent that all roads and lanes cut across Russian Zone of Occupation and due to the necessity of protecting these roads and lanes an extremely difficult administrative problem arises. Marshal Zhukov stated that one railway and one highway should be enough to feed and supply a small garrison of 50,000 troops, the overall combined figure of British and American occupying forces. He cannot agree to two air lines and suggests as substitute a route from Berlin through Magdeburg and Goslar. That would be 50 kilometers longer, which isn't too much flying. General Clay defended requests for several roads and two air lines. American sole port is Bremen in Northwest Germany, our occupation area is in Southwest Germany, and Berlin is the administrative occupation zone. It is necessary to have freedom of access and rights on roads and lanes. Americans have not asked for exclusive use of the roads and lanes, but must have rights to use them as we need. Marshal Zhukov stated he is not turning down the right but the Soviet authorities are not expected to give any corridor. If Americans do not like route through Magdeburg it can be changed but Marshal Zhukov chose Magdeburg route because it was a central lane, reasonable to both British and American forces. The railway and highway both go through Magdeburg and the central route would be most economical. General Clay asked only for right to move without restriction under whatever Russian regulations are set down. Marshal Zhukov asked if French will have any additional requirements to which General Clay replied that he didn't

---

[1] *Foreign Relations*, 1945, vol. III, pp. 353-361. The notes were made by General Floyd L. Parks, Commanding General, First Airborne Army. The conference was held at Marshal Zhukov's headquarters at 1430 hours.

think so, but British and Americans cannot speak for them. It was agreed to accept Magdeburg–Berlin railway, the gauge of which has not been changed and will not be changed without prior notice to British and Americans. Regarding Magdeburg bridge, it was agreed that it will be rebuilt with American material and Russian engineers. The British agreed not to make further demands for the Hamburg–Berlin railway. It was agreed to accept the autobahn Hannover–Magdeburg–Brandenburg–Berlin road for use by both British and American forces. Marshal Zhukov asked that U.S. forces release request for other roads. General Clay accepted the one road with right reserved to reopen question at the Control Council in the event that one road is not satisfactory. Marshal Zhukov stated that possibly all points discussed at this conference may be changed.

General Parks stated that movement of American occupying troops from Halle into Berlin will require at least two weeks. Marshal Zhukov said it was impossible for them to be delayed more than 4 days as the Soviets will be requiring the road for their own troop movement and supply. General Parks urged strongly to General Clay not to release the road from Halle to Berlin, but General Clay said he couldn't hold up negotiations for one short road. General Clay then stated that if the Halle-Berlin road were released, it would be necessary to have a staging area in Magdeburg which Marshal Zhukov said would not be objectionable. General Parks brought up question of Signal Communications stating that long lines—formerly German cables—have been put in shape and now are operating all the way from Frankfurt to Leipzig. They will be the main communication link to Frankfurt for the conference and must be serviced by American troops. Marshal Zhukov stated this question would be settled in discussion of next paragraph. General Clay asked for unlimited access to roads and Marshal Zhukov stated he did not understand just what the British and Americans desired. It will be necessary for vehicles to be governed by Russian road signs, military police, document checking, but no inspection of cargo—the Soviets are not interested in what is being hauled, how much, or how many trucks are moving. This was agreeable to all 3 Powers represented. The exchange of forces for occupation of Berlin and German territory west of Berlin will not have passes due to the imminence of the move. There were no objections to all points and agreement established.

Document A8

Decision of the Control Council Approving Establishment of Berlin–Hamburg, Berlin–Buckeburg (Hannover), and Berlin–Frankfurt-am-Main Air Corridors, November 30, 1945 [1]

[Extracts]

MINUTES OF THE THIRTEENTH MEETING HELD IN BERLIN, 30 NOVEMBER 1945 AT 1400 HOURS

There Were Present:

Marshal of the Soviet Union [Zhukov] (Chairman)
General McNarney
Field Marshal Montgomery
Lt. General Koenig

Others Present:

Soviet
Army General Sokolovsky
Minister Semenov
Col. General Serov
Major General Trusov

American
Lt. General Clay
Ambassador Murphy
Major General Echols
Brigadier General Milburn

British
Sir William Strang
Admiral Burrough
Lt. General Robertson
Air Marshal Wigglesworth
Maj. General Playfair

France
Lt. General Koeltz
Monsieur De La Tournelle

Secretariat   First Secretary Kudriavtsev
Major Kudriavtsev
Colonel Gerhardt
Colonel Birdsall
Brigadier Grazenbrook
Lt. Colonel Greenwood
Monsieur Calvy
Captain Joos

"110. Proposed Air Routes for Inter-Zonal Flights.

The Meeting had before them CONL/P(45)63.

Marshal Zhukov recalled that the Coordinating Committee had approved the establishing of three air corridors, namely, Berlin–Hamburg, Berlin–Buckeburg and Berlin–Frankfurt am Main.

Field Marshal Montgomery expressed the hope that in due course the question of establishing the remaining air corridors would be settled satisfactorily.

General Koenig approved the paper in principle and shared the opinion of Field Marshal Montgomery.

Marshal Zhukov expressed himself confident that in due course the other air corridors would be opened. He added that he would like to make a proposal on this paper. He assumed that his colleagues would give the Soviet military authorities the right to fly along these air corridors into the Western zones and would consent to put at their disposal appropriate airfields for landing Soviet aircraft, or at least allow Soviet grounds staffs on terminal and intermediate airfields along the proposed air corridors to facilitate the servicing of Soviet aircraft. The reason which Marshal Zhukov gave for the necessity of establishing Soviet airfields in the Western zones was the work of dismantling plants for deliveries on account of reparations when it comes to sending Soviet experts to organise that work.

Field Marshal Montgomery stated that in his zone he would afford every facility for Soviet aircraft.

Marshal Zhukov said that he would like to clarify his declaration: namely, he proposed that appropriate airfields should be placed at the disposal of the Soviet authorities in the Western zones, or that permission should be given for Soviet ground crews for the servicing of Soviet aircraft to be stationed at these airfields.

Field Marshal Montgomery proposed to refer the proposal made by the head of the Soviet delegation to the Air Directorate for examination. He asked whether his understanding was correct that the question of the three air corridors from the Western zones to Berlin was settled and that the organisation of these air corridors could be started immediately, without awaiting the results of the examination of Soviet proposal.

Marshal Zhukov observed that he considered the paper accepted and expressed the hope that the proposal of the Soviet delegation on placing airfields in the Western zones at the disposal of the Soviet authorities would meet with full sympathy on the part of his colleagues.

The Meeting

(110)(a) approved the establishment of three air corridors from Berlin to the Western zones as defined in CONL/P(45)63

(b) agreed to refer the proposal of the Soviet delegation on the placing of airfields at the disposal of the Soviet authorities or the setting up of Soviet ground crews in the Western zones to the Air Directorate for study."

Document A9

Revised Regulations Governing Flights in Air Corridors in Germany and the Berlin Control Zone, Issued by the Air Directorate, October 22, 1946 [1]

SECTION I

GENERAL

1. a. *Object.* To ensure the maximum safety in flight of all aircraft flying in corridors and in the Berlin Control Zone under all conditions.

b. *Definition.* Definitions of terms used in this paper are contained in Section V.

2. *Air Corridors in Germany.* The following air corridors have been established.

> FRANKFURT–BERLIN
> BUCKEBURG–BERLIN
> HAMBURG–BERLIN

Each of the above corridors is 20 English miles (32 kilometers) wide, i.e. 10 miles (16 kilometers) each side of the center line. It is probable that from time to time additional corridors may be established, and these rules apply equally to any such corridors.

3. *Berlin Control Zone (B.C.Z.)*

   a. The Berlin Control Zone is defined as the air space between ground level and 10,000 feet (3000 meters) within a radius of 20 miles (32 kilometers) from the Allied Control Authority Building in which is established the Berlin Air Safety Center (B.A.S.C.)

   b. The Berlin Control Zone is a zone of free flight for all aircraft entering the zone to land on the Berlin airfields or taking off to depart therefrom.

   c. It is desirable that, wherever possible, local flights (testing, training etc.) be executed above the national sectors. However, if necessary they may be executed above the remainder of the

---

[1] Doc. DAIR/P(45)71 Second Revise; text from Department of State press release, September 2, 1961.

Control Zone, subject to normal clearance by the Berlin Air Safety Center.

d. Owing to close proximity of the various national airfields within the Berlin Control Zone, Airdrome Traffic Zones are introduced with rules of procedure for safety of Allied aircraft while flying within the Berlin Control Zone.

1) "Airdrome Traffic Zone" is a designated zone to include the air space up to and including 2,650 feet (800 meters) and over the area having a radius of 2 miles from the center of the main traffic airfields in the Berlin Control Zone.
2) No aircraft will enter an airdrome traffic zone except for the purpose of landing at that airfield.

No Allied aircraft will approach an airfield, other than their own, closer than a radius of 2 miles, or at a height of less than 2,650 feet (800 meters) without having obtained prior permission from the Berlin Air Safety Center.

The above mentioned rules on airdrome traffic zones apply to the following airdromes of the Berlin Control Zone:

ADLERSHOF, DALGOW, ELSTHAL, GATOW, SCHOENEFELD, SCHOENEWALDE, TEMPELHOF, New French Airfield at FROHNAU (when in operation).

4. *Berlin Air Safety Center (B.A.S.C.).* The Berlin Air Safety Center has been established in the Allied Control Authority Building with the object of ensuring safety of flight for all aircraft in the Berlin area. The safety Center regulates all flying in the Berlin Control Zone and also in the corridors extending from Berlin to the boundaries of adjacent control zones. The functions of the Berlin Air Safety Center area as follows:

a. To maintain up-to-date information on the state of the weather over German territory and in other Control Zones.

b. To regulate air traffic in the Berlin Control Zones (in conditions of bad visibility and at night) by fixing the time, course, and height of flight, and ensuring the vertical and horizontal separation of aircraft necessary to avoid collision.

c. To inform crews of aircraft in or near the Berlin Control Zone of the weather conditions and the situation in the air, giving, if necessary, recommendations on courses to detour areas with bad meteorological conditions, or give routes in the limits of the Berlin Control Zone and other recommendations.

d. To receive information from airfields located in the Berlin Control Zone on aircraft landings thereon.

e. To coordinate search for aircraft on request by airfields in those cases where the aircraft is one or more hours overdue.

f. To be constantly informed of the conditions of airfields, radio facilities, and navigational and other aids for flight security, situated in the Berlin Control Zone.

g. To inform airfields located within the Berlin Control Zone about proposed landings of aircraft on them and to receive confirmation from those airfields about their readiness to accept arriving aircraft.

h. To receive information from airfields, and also from aircraft in flight about proposed flights over the Berlin Control Zone and about landings on airfields within the Zone.

i. To compile necessary operational and statistical reports.

j. To obtain clearance for aircraft wishing to proceed to other recognized Control Zones.

5. Control of aircraft traffic by the B.A.S.C. is normally exercised through the appropriate national airfields in the Berlin Control Zone.

6. *Aircraft Flying to and from Berlin Under Visual Flight Rules (VFR).*

a. Arriving aircraft will contact the airfield of destination in the Berlin Control Zone at a distance of 75 miles (120 kilometers) from Berlin, giving their estimated time of arrival, altitude and other information as appears necessary. (The communications contact is not mandatory but is desirable). The airfield at which the aircraft arrives will inform the B.A.S.C. of such arrival.

b. Departing Aircraft. The airfield clearing departing aircraft in Berlin Control Zone will inform the B.A.S.C. of each departure.

c. Aircraft without two-way radio or whose radio has failed are free to fly into or out of the Berlin Control Zone in accordance with Visual Flight Rules (Section III).

d. When aircraft are departing to another Control Zone, the airfield of departure will obtain clearance through B.A.S.C. in case Instrument Flight Rules are in force at the airfield of destination. Should this be the case, the B.A.S.C. will obtain clearance from the Control Zones at destination.

7. *Aircraft Flying to and from the Berlin Control Zone Under Instrument Flight Rules (IFR)*

a. Aircraft flying into and out of the Berlin Control Zone will operate under Instrument Flight Rules (IFR) (Section IV) when the visibility is less than 3 miles (5 kilometers) or the ceiling is less than 1000 feet (300 meters).

b. Incoming aircraft will be required to contact by radio the airfield of destination when not less than 75 miles (120 kilometers) from the Berlin Control Zone. Airfield of destination will inform B.A.S.C. accordingly, which will issue an air traffic clearance and such other information and instructions as appear necessary for safety.

c. All landings, under instrument flight conditions, will be controlled by the airfield of destination, which will have previously obtained all necessary instruction and information from B.A.S.C.

d. Departing aircraft must be cleared through B.A.S.C. which will approve the flight plan as filed or indicate such changes as may be necessary to ensure adequate separation.

8. *Aircraft Crossing Corridors.* Aircraft will call whenever possible, the appropriate communications station, and obtain clearance prior to crossing a corridor. When aircraft are unable to receive clearance to cross corridors, they will cross at a magnetic heading of 90 degrees to that corridor and at an altitude appropriate to the quadrant in which the heading lies. (See para. 26).

SECTION II

GENERAL FLIGHT RULES

9. Aircraft shall be flown at all times in compliance with the rules contained in this Section and in addition shall comply with either the Visual Flight Rules or the Instrument Flight Rules.

10. *Preflight Action.* Prior to commencing a flight, the person in command of an aircraft shall familiarize himself with information necessary for the proper operation of the aircraft enroute and on the airfields which may be used.

11. *Airspace Restrictions.* Aircraft shall not be flown over areas, particulars of which have been duly published and where flight is restricted by a state, except in accordance with the terms of such permission as may be granted by the appropriate authority.

12. *Reckless Flying.* An aircraft shall not be operated in a negligent manner or in a reckless manner so as to endanger life or property of others.

13. *Landing and Take-off Rules.* The person in command of an aircraft operated on or in the vicinity of an airfield shall comply with the following rules:

a. Observe other airfield traffic for the purpose of avoiding collision.

b. Conform to or avoid the pattern of traffic formed by other aircraft in operation.

c. Make all turns to the left, when approaching for a landing and after taking off, unless otherwise prescribed by the appropriate authority or instructed by airfield control.

d. If airfield control is in operation—

(1) Maintain a continuous watch on the appropriate radio channel, or if this is not possible, keep a watch for such instructions as may be issued by visual means.

(2) Obtain, either by radio or visual signal, such authorization for his movements as may be necessary for the protection of airfield traffic.

e. If airfield control is not in operation, landing and taking off shall, insofar as practicable, be into the wind.

14. *Air Traffic Control Instructions.* The person in command of an aircraft operated in areas where air traffic control is exercised shall comply with Air Traffic control instructions received.

15. *Right-of-Way Rules.*

a. *General.*   65

(1) An aircraft shall not be operated in such a proximity to other aircraft as to create a collision hazard. Flight in formation is prohibited. An aircraft which is obliged by the following rules to keep out of the way of another shall avoid passing over or under the other, or crossing ahead of it, unless passing well clear of it.

(2) The aircraft which has the right-of-way shall normally maintain its course and speed; nevertheless, nothing in these rules shall absolve the person in command of an aircraft from taking such action as will best aid to avert collision.

(3) *Proximity.* Aircraft shall be flown at least 500 feet (150 meters) apart except by pre-arrangement of the pilot in command of the aircraft.

(4) Aircraft flying in the corridors must fly straight, at a height in accordance with Flight Rules, and not perform acrobatics.

b. *Converging.*

(1) An aircraft shall give way to another aircraft in a class different from its own in the following order:

(a) mechanically-driven aircraft;
(b) airships;
(c) gliders;
(d) balloons.

(2) When two aircraft of the same class are at approximately the same altitude, the aircraft which has the other on its right shall give way; nevertheless, mechanically-driven aircraft shall give way to aircraft which are seen to be towing another aircraft.

c. *Approaching Head-on.* When two aircraft are approaching head-on, or approximately so and there is danger of collision, each shall alter its course to the right, as soon as visible to each other, and at a distance not less than 1,500 feet (500 meters).

d. *Overtaking.* An aircraft which is being overtaken has the right-of-way, and the overtaking aircraft, whether climbing, descending or in horizontal flight, shall keep out of the way of the other aircraft by altering its course to the right, and no subsequent change in the relative positions of the two aircraft shall absolve the overtaking aircraft from this obligation until it is entirely past and clear. This alteration of course should be made when the overtaking aircraft is not less than one mile (1,500 meters) from the overtaking aircraft.

NOTE: An overtaking aircraft is an aircraft which approaches another from the rear on a line forming an angle of less than 70 degrees with the plane of symmetry of the latter, i.e., is in such a position with reference to the other aircraft that at night it should be unable to see either of that aircraft's forward lights.

e. *Landing.*

(1) Aircraft, while landing or maneuvering in preparation to land, have the right-of-way over other aircraft in flight or on the ground or water.

(2) In the case of two or more mechanically-driven aircraft approaching an airfield for the purpose of landing, the aircraft at the lower altitude has the right-of-way, but it shall not take advantage of this rule to cut in in front of another which is descending in a straight line for the purpose of landing, or to overtake that aircraft.

f. *Taking off.* An aircraft about to take off shall not attempt to do so until there is no apparent risk of collision with another aircraft.

g. *Emergency Landing.* An aircraft which is aware that another is compelled to land shall give way to that aircraft.

16. *Minimum Safe Altitudes*—Except when necessary for taking off and landing in an emergency or when otherwise ordered, aircraft shall be flown;

a. When over the congested areas of cities, towns, settlements, or open air assemblies of persons, at altitudes sufficient to permit emergency landings outside such areas and in no cases less than 1,000 feet (300 meters) above such areas.

(b) When elsewhere than as specified in paragraph (a), at an altitude of not less than 500 feet (150 meters).

17. *Towing Objects.* The person in command of an aircraft shall not permit anything to be towed by such an aircraft, except in accordance with requirements prescribed by the appropriate authority.

18. *Dropping Objects.* The person in command of an aircraft shall not permit anything to be dropped from the aircraft in flight which might create hazard to person or property on the ground or water.

19. *Parachute Descents.* Parachute descents, other than necessary emergency descents, shall not be made unless authorized by the appropriate authority.

20. *Acrobatic Flight.* No aircraft shall be acrobatically flown so as to endanger air traffic; furthermore, the performance of acrobatics over certain areas may be subject to the consent of the appropriate authority.

21. *Additional Rules for Night Operations.*

a. *Lights.*

(1) Aircraft in Operation—By night all aircraft being operated shall display lights.

(2) Aircraft Not in Operation—By night all airfields used or available for night flying, all aircraft parked or moving on the Movement Area or in dangerous proximity thereto, shall be clearly illuminated or lighted or the area which they occupy marked with obstruction lights.

b. *Flights within Control Areas or Control Zones.* All aircraft being operated at night within control areas or control zones

shall be flown in accordance with the Instrument Flight Rules
or as otherwise authorized by B.A.S.C. or other Air Traffic
Center.

22. *Authority of Person in Command of an Aircraft.* The person
in command of an aircraft shall be directly responsible for its operation and shall have final authority as to disposition of the aircraft
while he is in command, which shall include the maintaining of
discipline of all persons on board.

23. *Notification of Arrival.* A person in command of an aircraft
making a flight for which a Flight Plan has been filed shall be responsible for ensuring that an arrival message is submitted immediately upon landing for transmission to the appropriate agency.

SECTION III

VISUAL FLIGHT RULES (VFR)

24. *Within Control Zones.* An aircraft operated within a Control
Zone shall be flown at least 2,000 feet (600 meters) horizontally and
500 feet (150 meters) vertically from all clouds, and with a flight
visibility of at least 3 statute miles (5 kilometers), unless

>   a. Otherwise authorized by B.A.S.C. or other Air Traffic
>   Center or
>   b. Flown in accordance with Instrument Flight Rules.

25. *Within Corridors and Control Areas but outside of Control
Zones.*

>   a. *At or above 700 feet (200 meters) above the ground or
>   water—*Aircraft shall be flown in accordance with the rules ap-
>   plicable to flight within control zones.
>   b. *Below 700 feet (200 meters) above the ground or water—*
>   Aircraft shall be flown out of clouds and within sight of the
>   ground or water.

26. *Quadrantal Height Separation.* Unless otherwise ordered aircraft flying in the Berlin Control Zone or in the corridors leading
to it will fly according to Quadrantal Height separations as set out
below, although this will not be mandatory except under Instrument Flight conditions. In order to avoid confusion the quandran-
tal heights applicable to each corridor are set out in para. 40.

Magnetic Heading	*Cruising Altitude (feet above sea level)*
From 0° up to but not includ-ing 90°	Odd thousands of feet (1000 and 3000 etc.)
From 90° up to but not includ-ing 180°	Odd thousands of feet plus 500 feet (1500, 3500, etc.)
From 180° up to but not in-cluding 270°	Even thousands of feet (2000, 4000 etc.)

From 270° up to but not in-   Even thousands of feet plus
cluding 360°   500 ft. (2500, 4500 etc.)

Section IV

INSTRUMENT FLIGHT RULES (IFR)

27. Aircraft within corridors or within the Berlin Control Zone shall be flown in accordance with the rules contained in this section except as provided in the Visual Flight Rules.

28. *Pilot Qualification.* The person in command of an aircraft shall be qualified for flight under Instrument Flight Rules.

29. *Aircraft Equipment.* Aircraft shall be equipped for IFR Flight to include:

    a. Suitable flight instruments.

    b. Radio Equipment so as to maintain two-way communication with B.A.S.C. or other Air Traffic Centers.

    c. Radio navigation equipment appropriate to the route to be flown.

30. *Altimeter.* At least one sensitive altimeter in each aircraft will be set to current pressure at mean sea level of the area in which the aircraft is flying.

31. *Fuel Requirements.* No aircraft shall take off without fuel and oil sufficient, considering the wind and other weather conditions forecast for the flight at least:

    a. To complete such flight to the point of first intended landing, and thereafter.

    b. To fly to and land at the alternate airfield designated in the flight plan, and thereafter.

    c. To fly, at normal cruising consumption, for a period of at least 45 minutes.

32. *Weather Minima.* Landing and take-off minima at their stations will be established by each agency operating aircraft in Europe.

33. *Alternate Airfield.* No take-off of aircraft will be made unless:

    a. The Alternate Airfield named in the flight plan has a landing area suitable for the aircraft to be used, and

    b. Weather reports and forecasts indicate that the weather conditions at the alternate airport will remain at or above the minima specified by the operating agency until the arrival of the aircraft thereat.

34. *Over-the-top Flight.* Such flight shall be governed by Instrument Flight Rules whenever the altitude of the aircraft and the flight path cannot be controlled at all times by visual reference to the ground or water.

35. *Preflight Action.* Prior to commencing a flight, the person in command of an aircraft shall make a careful study of available current weather reports and forecasts and shall determine that the flight can be made with safety, taking into consideration fuel re-

quirements and alternate course of action in the event that flight cannot be completed as planned.

36. *Flight Plan.* Prior to take-off from any point within or prior to entering a Control Area or Control Zone, a Flight Plan shall be filed with the appropriate Air Traffic Center (B.A.S.C.). Such Flight Plan shall contain the following information unless otherwise authorized by B.A.S.C. or Air Traffic Center.

> a. The aircraft identification and radio call sign;
> b. The type of aircraft involved;
> c. The name of the person in command of the aircraft;
> d. The point of departure;
> e. The cruising altitude, or altitude, and the route to be followed;
> f. The point of first intended landing;
> g. The proposed true air speed at cruising altitude;
> h. Transmitting and receiving frequency or frequencies to be used;
> i. The proposed time of departure, or entry in Control Area or Control Zone;
> j. The estimated elapsed time until arrival over the point of first intended landing;
> k. The alternate airfield;
> l. The amount of fuel on board expressed in hours;
> m. Any other pertinent information which the person in command of the aircraft, or the Air Traffic Center, deems necessary for control purposes.

37. *Air Traffic Clearance.* Prior to operating an Aircraft in a Control Area or a Control Zone, a traffic clearance based on the flight plan shall be obtained from the appropriate Air Traffic Center. Aircraft shall be flown in accordance with an air traffic clearance and, where applicable, shall follow the published instrument approach procedure for the airfields to be used. No deviations shall be made from the requirements of an air traffic clearance unless an emergency situation arises which necessitates immediate action, in which case as soon as possible after such emergency authority is exercised, the person in command of the aircraft shall inform the appropriate Air Traffic Center of the deviation and, if necessary, obtain an amended clearance.

38. *Communication Contacts.* When the flight is made within Control Areas or Control Zones, the person in command of an aircraft shall be responsible for ensuring that a continuous listening watch is maintained on the appropriate radio frequency and that the time and altitude of passing each designated point, together with any other required information, are reported by radio as soon as possible to the appropriate Air Traffic Center.

39. *Communication Failure.* In the event of inability to maintain two-way radio communication as required by Paragraph 38 above, the person in command of an aircraft shall observe one of the following procedures in the order listed:

> a. Proceed according to current air traffic clearance, or, if not received, according to Flight Plan, and commence descent

at destination at approach time last authorized, or, if not received, at the estimated time of arrival specified in Flight Plan;

b. Proceed in weather conditions equal to or better than those specified in the Visual Flight Rules;

c. Land as soon as practicable.

40. *Corridor Cruising Altitudes*

a. Except when necessary for taking off or landing, aircraft operating in a Corridor shall be flown at not less than 1000 feet (300 meters) above the surface.

b. Aircraft operating in the corridors shall fly at the cruising altitudes indicated below:

From	To		Cruising
Berlin	Frankfurt	Even thousands feet	(Even multiples of 300 m)
Frankfurt	Berlin	Odd thousands feet	(Odd multiples of 300 m)
Berlin	Buckeburg	Even thousands +500 feet	(Even multiples of 300 m +150 m)
Buckeburg	Berlin	Odd thousands +500 feet	(Odd multiples of 300 m +500 m)
Berlin	Hamburg	Even thousands +500 feet	(Even multiples of 300 m +150 m)
Hamburg	Berlin	Odd thousands +500 feet	(Odd multiples of 300 m +150 m)

[SECTION V: DEFINITIONS]

41. *Acrobatic Flight.* Maneuvers intentionally performed by an aircraft involving an abrupt change in its attitude, an abnormal attitude, or an abnormal speed.

42. *Airfield Traffic.* Aircraft operating on and in the vicinity of an airfield.

43. *Airfield.* A defined area on land or water including any buildings or installations, normally used for the take-off and landing (alighting) of aircraft.

44. *Airfield Control.* A service established to provide air traffic control for airfields.

45. *Air Traffic.* Aircraft operation anywhere in the airspace and on the movement area of an airfield.

46. *Air Traffic Clearance.* Authorization by Air Traffic Control for an aircraft to proceed under specified conditions.

47. *Air Traffic Center.* An agency established to promote the safe, orderly and expeditious flow of air traffic.

48. *Air Traffic Control Area.* (See *Corridor*)

49. *Air Traffic Control Zone.* (See *Control Zone*)

50. *Air Traffic Controller.* A person responsible for the control of air traffic while on duty at an Air Traffic Center (Air Safety Center).

51. *Alternate Airfield.* An airfield specified in the Flight Plan to which a flight may proceed when a landing at the intended destination becomes inadvisable.

52. *Approach Time.* The time at which an aircraft is expected to commence its approach procedure preparatory to landing.

53. *Airway Communications Station.* A radio, teletype, or other communications station.

54. *Cloud Ceiling.* Cloud ceiling is the distance in feet from ground level to the base of the clouds.

55. *Control Tower.* A facility established at an airfield to provide Airfield Control Service.

56. *Control Area.* An airspace of defined dimensions designated by the appropriate authorities to embrace corridor control zones, or similar areas.

57. *Control Zone.* An airspace of defined dimensions designated by the appropriate authorities to include one or more aerodromes and within which rules additional to those governing flight in control areas apply for the protection of air traffic against collision.

58. *Cruising Altitude.* A constant altimeter indication maintained during a flight or portion thereof.

59. *Flight Plan.* Specified information relative to the intended navigation of an aircraft.

60. *Flight Visibility.* The pilot's average range of vision, except for landing and taking off at a location where there is an accredited observer, in which case the visibility shall be that reported by such observer.

61. *IFR.* The symbol used internationally to designate the term "Instrument Flight Rules."

62. *IFR Flight.* The flight of an aircraft conducted in accordance with Instrument Flight Rules under conditions of visibilities or cloud ceilings lower than the minima prescribed in Rules of the Air for Visual Flight.

63. *Movement Area.* The part of an airfield reserved for the taking off, landing and maneuvering of aircraft. (Landing, Take off, and Taxiing Area).

64. *Night.* The hours of darkness between sunset and sunrise or such other period between sunset and sunrise as may be prescribed by the appropriate authority.

65. *Reporting Point.* A geographical location, in relation to which the position of an aircraft is to be reported.

66. *Visual Flight.* The flight of an aircraft in which the attitude and its flight path can at all times be controlled by means of visual reference to the earth's surface.

67. *VFR.* The symbol used internationally to designate the term "Visual Flight Rules."

68. *VFR Flight.* The flight of an aircraft conducted in accordance with Visual Flight Rules under conditions of visibilities or cloud ceilings at or above the minima prescribed in Rules of the Air for Visual Flight.

69. *Traffic Clearance.* An approval of a flight or portion thereof by an Air Traffic Center of Control Tower with regard only to prevention of collision between aircraft whose movements are known.

70. *Visibility.* The greatest mean distance measured horizontally at which conspicuous objects can be seen and identified with the normal eye.

Document A10

Four-Power Communiqué on Arrangements for Lifting the Berlin Blockade Effective May 12, New York, May 4, 1949 [1]

The Governments of France, the Union of Soviet Socialist Republics, the United Kingdom, and the United States have reached the following agreement:

1. All the restrictions imposed since March 1, 1948 by the Government of the Union of Soviet Socialist Republics on communications, transportation, and trade between Berlin and the Western zones of Germany and between the Eastern zone and the Western zones will be removed on May 12, 1949.

2. All the restrictions imposed since March 1, 1948 by the Governments of France, the United Kingdom, and the United States, or any one of them, on communication, transportation, and trade between Berlin and the Eastern zone and between the Western and Eastern zones of Germany will also be removed on May 12, 1949.

3. Eleven days subsequent to the removal of the restrictions referred to in paragraphs one and two, namely, on May 23, 1949, a meeting of the Council of Foreign Ministers will be convened in Paris to consider questions relating to Germany and problems arising out of the situation in Berlin, including also the question of currency in Berlin.

Document A11

Quadripartite Agreement on Berlin, Signed at Berlin, September 3, 1971 [1]

The Governments of the United States of America, the French Republic, the Union of Soviet Socialist Republics and the United Kingdom of Great Britain and Northern Ireland,

---

[1] Department of State *Bulletin*, September 27, 1971, pp. 318–322. In addition to the documents printed here and below, representatives of the Four Powers also initialed on September 3 a Draft Protocol on the Entry into Force of the Quadripartite Agreement on Berlin, which was the same as that formally signed on June 3, 1972. See *post*.

Represented by their Ambassadors, who held a series of meetings in the building formerly occupied by the Allied Control Council in the American Sector of Berlin,

Acting on the basis of their quadripartite rights and responsibilities, and of the corresponding wartime and postwar agreements and decisions of the Four Powers, which are not affected,

Taking into account the existing situation in the relevant area,

Guided by the desire to contribute to practical improvements of the situation,

Without prejudice to their legal positions,

Have agreed on the following:

PART I

GENERAL PROVISIONS

1. The four Governments will strive to promote the elimination of tension and the prevention of complications in the relevant area.

2. The four Governments, taking into account their obligations under the Charter of the United Nations, agree that there shall be no use or threat of force in the area and that disputes shall be settled solely by peaceful means.

3. The four Governments will mutually respect their individual and joint rights and responsibilities, which remain unchanged.

4. The four Governments agree that, irrespective of the differences in legal views, the situation which has developed in the area, and as it is defined in this Agreement as well as in the other agreements referred to in this Agreement, shall not be changed unilaterally.

PART II

PROVISIONS RELATING TO THE WESTERN SECTORS OF BERLIN

A. The Government of the Union of Soviet Socialist Republics declares that transit traffic by road, rail and waterways through the territory of the German Democratic Republic of civilian persons and goods between the Western Sectors of Berlin and the Federal Republic of Germany will be unimpeded; that such traffic will be facilitated so as to take place in the most simple and expeditious manner; and that it will receive preferential treatment.

Detailed arrangements concerning this civilian traffic, as set forth in Annex I, will be agreed by the competent German authorities.

B. The Governments of the French Republic, the United Kingdom and the United States of America declare that the ties between the Western Sectors of Berlin and the Federal Republic of Germany will be maintained and developed, taking into account that these Sectors continue not to be a constituent part of the Federal Republic of Germany and not to be governed by it.

Detailed arrangements concerning the relationship between the Western Sectors of Berlin and the Federal Republic of Germany are set forth in Annex II.

C. The Government of the Union of Soviet Socialist Republics declares that communications between the Western Sectors of Berlin and areas bordering on these Sectors and those areas of the German Democratic Republic which do not border on these Sectors will be improved. Permanent residents of the Western Sectors of Berlin will be able to travel to and visit such areas for compassionate, family, religious, cultural or commercial reasons, or as tourists, under conditions comparable to those applying to other persons entering these areas.

The problems of the small enclaves, including Steinstuecken, and of other small areas may be solved by exchange of territory.

Detailed arrangements concerning travel, communications and the exchange of territory, as set forth in Annex III, will be agreed by the competent German authorities.

D. Representation abroad of the interests of the Western Sectors of Berlin and consular activities of the Union of Soviet Socialist Republics in the Western Sectors of Berlin can be exercised as set forth in Annex IV.

Part III

Final Provisions

This Quadripartite Agreement will enter into force on the date specified in a Final Quadripartite Protocol to be concluded when the measures envisaged in Part II of this Quadripartite Agreement and in its Annexes have been agreed.

Done at the building formerly occupied by the Allied Control Council in the American Sector of Berlin this 3rd day of September 1971, in four originals, each in the English, French and Russian languages, all texts being equally authentic.

For the Government of the United States of America:
KENNETH RUSH.

For the Government of the French Republic:
JEAN SAUVAGNARGUES.

For the Government of the Union of Soviet Socialist Republics:
PYOTE A. ABRASIMOV.

For the Government of the United Kingdom of Great Britain and Northern Ireland:
ROGER JACKLING.

Annex I

COMMUNICATION FROM THE GOVERNMENT OF THE UNION OF SOVIET SOCIALIST REPUBLICS TO THE GOVERNMENTS OF THE FRENCH REPUBLIC, THE UNITED KINGDOM AND THE UNITED STATES OF AMERICA

The Government of the Union of Soviet Socialist Republics, with reference to Part II(A) of the Quadripartite Agreement of this date and after consultation and agreement with the Government of the German Democratic Republic, has the honor to inform the Governments of the French Republic, the United Kingdom and the United States of America that:

1. Transit traffic by road, rail and waterways through the territory of the German Democratic Republic of civilian persons and goods between the Western Sectors of Berlin and the Federal Republic of Germany will be facilitated and unimpeded. It will receive the most simple, expeditious and preferential treatment provided by international practice.

2. Accordingly,

(a) Conveyances sealed before departure may be used for the transport of civilian goods by road, rail and waterways between the Western Sectors of Berlin and the Federal Republic of Germany. Inspection procedures will be limited to the inspection of seals and accompanying documents.

(b) With regard to conveyances which cannot be sealed, such as open trucks, inspection procedures will be limited to the inspection of accompanying documents. In special cases where there is sufficient reason to suspect that unsealed conveyances contain either material intended for dissemination along the designated routes or persons or material put on board along these routes, the content of unsealed conveyances may be inspected. Procedures for dealing with such cases will be agreed by the competent German authorities.

(c) Through trains and buses may be used for travel between the Western Sectors of Berlin and the Federal Republic of Germany. Inspection procedures will not include any formalities other than identification of persons.

(d) Persons identified as through travellers using individual vehicles between the Western Sectors of Berlin and the Federal Republic of Germany on routes designated for through traffic will be able to proceed to their destinations without paying individual tolls and fees for the use of the transit routes. Procedures applied for such travellers shall not involve delay. The travellers, their vehicles and personal baggage will not be subject to search, detention or exclusion from use of the designated routes, except in special cases, as may be agreed by the competent German authorities, where there is sufficient reason to suspect that misuse of the transit routes is intended for purposes not related to direct travel to and from the Western Sectors of Berlin and contrary to generally applicable regulations concerning public order.

(e) Appropriate compensation for fees and tolls and for other costs related to traffic on the communication routes between the Western Sectors of Berlin and the Federal Republic of Germany, including the maintenance of adequate routes, facilities and installations used for such traffic, may be made in the form of an annual lump sum paid to the German Democratic Republic by the Federal Republic of Germany.

3. Arrangements implementing and supplementing the provisions of paragraphs 1 and 2 above will be agreed by the competent German authorities.

Annex II

COMMUNICATION FROM THE GOVERNMENTS OF THE FRENCH REPUBLIC, THE UNITED KINGDOM AND THE UNITED STATES OF AMERICA TO THE GOVERNMENT OF THE UNION OF SOVIET SOCIALIST REPUBLICS

The Governments of the French Republic, the United Kingdom and the United States of America, with reference to Part II(B) of the Quadripartite Agreement of this date and after consultation with the Government of the Federal Republic of Germany, have the honor to inform the Government of the Union of Soviet Socialist Republics that:

1. They declare, in the exercise of their rights and responsibilities, that the ties between the Western Sectors of Berlin and the Federal Republic of Germany will be maintained and developed, taking into account that these Sectors continue not to be a constituent part of the Federal Republic of Germany and not to be governed by it. The provisions of the Basic Law of the Federal Republic of Germany and of the Constitution operative in the Western Sectors of Berlin which contradict the above have been suspended and continue not to be in effect.

2. The Federal President, the Federal Government, the Bundesversammlung, the Bundesrat and the Bundestag, including their Committees and Fraktionen, as well as other state bodies of the Federal Republic of Germany will not perform in the Western Sectors of Berlin constitutional or official acts which contradict the provisions of paragraph 1.

3. The Government of the Federal Republic of Germany will be represented in the Western Sectors of Berlin to the authorities of the three Governments and to the Senat by a permanent liaison agency.

Annex III

COMMUNICATION FROM THE GOVERNMENT OF THE UNION OF SOVIET SOCIALIST REPUBLICS TO THE GOVERNMENTS OF THE FRENCH REPUBLIC, THE UNITED KINGDOM AND THE UNITED STATES OF AMERICA

The Government of the Union of Soviet Socialist Republics, with reference to Part II(C) of the Quadripartite Agreement of this date and after consultation and agreement with the Government of the German Democratic Republic, has the honor to inform the Governments of the French Republic, the United Kingdom and the United States of America that:

1. Communications between the Western Sectors of Berlin and areas bordering on these Sectors and those areas of the German Democratic Republic which do not border on these Sectors will be improved.

2. Permanent residents of the Western Sectors of Berlin will be able to travel to and visit such areas for compassionate, family, religious, cultural or commercial reasons, or as tourists, under conditions comparable to those applying to other persons entering these areas. In order to facilitate visits and travel, as described above, by permanent residents of the Western Sectors of Berlin, additional crossing points will be opened.

3. The problems of the small enclaves, including Steinstuecken, and of other small areas may be solved by exchange of territory.

4. Telephonic, telegraphic, transport and other external communications of the Western Sectors of Berlin will be expanded.

5. Arrangements implementing and supplementing the provisions of paragraphs 1 to 4 above will be agreed by the competent German authorities.

Annex IV

A. COMMUNICATION FROM THE GOVERNMENTS OF THE FRENCH REPUBLIC, THE UNITED KINGDOM AND THE UNITED STATES OF AMERICA TO THE GOVERNMENT OF THE UNION OF SOVIET SOCIALIST REPUBLICS

The Governments of the French Republic, the United Kingdom and the United States of America, with reference to Part II (D) of the Quadripartite Agreement of this date and after consultation with the Government of the Federal Republic of Germany, have the honor to inform the Government of the Union of Soviet Socialist Republics that:

1. The Governments of the French Republic, the United Kingdom and the United States of America maintain their rights and responsibilities relating to the representation abroad of the interests of the Western Sectors of Berlin and their permanent residents, including those rights and responsibilities concerning matters of security and status, both in international organizations and in relations with other countries.

2. Without prejudice to the above and provided that matters of security and status are not affected, they have agreed that:

(a) The Federal Republic of Germany may perform consular services for permanent residents of the Western Sectors of Berlin.

(b) In accordance with established procedures, international agreements and arrangements entered into by the Federal Republic of Germany may be extended to the Western Sectors of

Berlin provided that the extension of such agreements and arrangements is specified in each case.

(c) The Federal Republic of Germany may represent the interests of the Western Sectors of Berlin in international organizations and international conferences.

(d) Permanent residents of the Western Sectors of Berlin may participate jointly with participants from the Federal Republic of Germany in international exchanges and exhibitions. Meetings of international organizations and international conferences as well as exhibitions with international participation may be held in the Western Sectors of Berlin. Invitations will be issued by the Senat or jointly by the Federal Republic of Germany and the Senat.

3. The three Governments authorize the establishment of a Consulate General of the USSR in the Western Sectors of Berlin accredited to the appropriate authorities of the three Governments in accordance with the usual procedures applied in those Sectors, for the purpose of performing consular services, subject to provisions set forth in a separate document of this date.

B. COMMUNICATION FROM THE GOVERNMENT OF THE UNION OF SOVIET SOCIALIST REPUBLICS TO THE GOVERNMENTS OF THE FRENCH REPUBLIC, THE UNITED KINGDOM AND THE UNITED STATES OF AMERICA

The Government of the Union of Soviet Socialist Republics, with reference to Part II(D) of the Quadripartite Agreement of this date and to the communication of the Governments of the French Republic, the United Kingdom and the United States of America with regard to the representation abroad of the interests of the Western Sectors of Berlin and their permanent residents, has the honor to inform the Governments of the French Republic, the United Kingdom and the United States of America that:

1. The Government of the Union of Soviet Socialist Republics takes note of the fact that the three Governments maintain their rights and responsibilities relating to the representation abroad of the interests of the Western Sectors of Berlin and their permanent residents, including those rights and responsibilities concerning matters of security and status, both in international organizations and in relations with other countries.

2. Provided that matters of security and status are not affected, for its part it will raise no objection to:

(a) the performance by the Federal Republic of Germany of consular services for permanent residents of the Western Sectors of Berlin;

(b) in accordance with established procedures, the extension to the Western Sectors of Berlin of international agreements and arrangements entered into by the Federal Republic of Germany provided that the extension of such agreements and arrangements is specified in each case;

(c) the representation of the interests of the Western Sectors of Berlin by the Federal Republic of Germany in international organizations and international conferences;

(d) the participation jointly with participants from the Federal Republic of Germany of permanent residents of the Western Sectors of Berlin in international exchanges and exhibitions, or the holding in those Sectors of meetings of international organizations and international conferences as well as exhibitions with international participation, taking into account that invitations will be issued by the Senat or jointly by the Federal Republic of Germany and the Senat.

3. The Government of the Union of Soviet Socialist Republics takes note of the fact that the three Governments have given their consent to the establishment of a Consulate General of the USSR in the Western Sectors of Berlin. It will be accredited to the appropriate authorities of the three Governments, for purposes and subject to provisions described in their communication and as set forth in a separate document of this date.

Agreed Minute I [2]

It is understood that permanent residents of the Western Sectors of Berlin shall, in order to receive at appropriate Soviet offices visas for entry into the Union of Soviet Socialist Republics, present:

(a) a passport stamped "Issued in accordance with the Quadripartite Agreement of September 3, 1971";

(b) an identity card or other appropriately drawn up document confirming that the person requesting the visa is a permanent resident of the Western Sectors of Berlin and containing the bearer's full address and a personal photograph.

During his stay in the Union of Soviet Socialist Republics, a permanent resident of the Western Sectors of Berlin who has received a visa in this way may carry both documents or either of them, as he chooses. The visa issued by a Soviet office will serve as the basis for entry into the Union of Soviet Socialist Republics, and the passport or identity card will serve as the basis for consular services in accordance with the Quadripartite Agreement during the stay of that person in the territory of the Union of Soviet Socialist Republics.

The above-mentioned stamp will appear in all passports used by permanent residents of the Western Sectors of Berlin for journeys to such countries as may require it.

Agreed Minute II [3]

Provision is hereby made for the establishment of a Consulate General of the USSR in the Western Sectors of Berlin. It is understood that the details concerning this Consulate General will include the following. The Consulate General will be accredited to the appropriate authorities of the three Governments in accord-

---

[2] Initialed by the four Ambassadors on September 3. [Footnote in the source text.]
[3] Initialed by the four Ambassadors on September 3. [Footnote in the source text.]

ance with the usual procedures applying in those Sectors. Applicable Allied and German legislation and regulations will apply to the Consulate General. The activities of the Consulate General will be of a consular character and will not include political functions or any matters related to quadripartite rights or responsibilities.

The three Governments are willing to authorize an increase in Soviet commercial activities in the Western Sectors of Berlin as described below. It is understood that pertinent Allied and German legislation and regulations will apply to these activities. This authorization will be extended indefinitely, subject to compliance with the provisions outlined herein. Adequate provision for consultation will be made. This increase will include establishment of an "Office of Soviet Foreign Trade Associations in the Western Sectors of Berlin", with commercial status, authorized to buy and sell on behalf of foreign trade associations of the Union of Soviet Socialist Republics. Soyuzpushnina, Prodintorg and Novoexport may each establish a bonded warehouse in the Western Sectors of Berlin to provide storage and display for their goods. The activities of the Intourist office in the British Sector of Berlin may be expanded to include the sale of tickets and vouchers for travel and tours in the Union of Soviet Socialist Republics and other countries. An office of Aeroflot may be established for the sale of passenger tickets and air freight services.

The assignment of personnel to the Consulate General and to permitted Soviet commercial organizations will be subject to agreement with the appropriate authorities of the three Governments. The number of such personnel will not exceed twenty Soviet nationals in the Consulate General; twenty in the office of the Soviet Foreign Trade Associations; one each in the bonded warehouses; six in the Intourist office; and five in the Aeroflot office. The personnel of the Consulate General and of permitted Soviet commercial organizations and their dependents may reside in the Western Sectors of Berlin upon individual authorization.

The property of the Union of Soviet Socialist Republics at Lietzenburgerstrasse 11 and at Am Sandwerder 1 may be used for purposes to be agreed between appropriate representatives of the three Governments and of the Government of the Union of Soviet Socialist Republics.

Details of implementation of the measures above and a time schedule for carrying them out will be agreed between the four Ambassadors in the period between the signature of the Quadripartite Agreement and the signature of the Final Quadripartite Protocol envisaged in that Agreement.

Document A12

Final Quadripartite Protocol on Berlin, Signed at Berlin, June 3, 1972 [1]

The Governments of the Union of Soviet Socialist Republics, the United Kingdom of Great Britain and Northern Ireland, the United States of America and the French Republic,

Having in mind Part III of the Quadripartite Agreement of September 3, 1971,[2] and taking note with satisfaction of the fact that the agreements and arrangements mentioned below have been concluded,
Have agreed on the following:

1. The four Governments, by virtue of this Protocol, bring into force the Quadripartite Agreement, which, like this Protocol, does not affect quadripartite agreements or decisions previously concluded or reached.
2. The four Governments proceed on the basis that the following agreements and arrangements concluded between the competent German authorities (list of agreements and arrangements)[3] shall enter into force simultaneously with the Quadripartite Agreement.

---

[1] *Documentation Relating to the Federal Government's Policy of Detente*, pp. 109–110.

[2] *Ante.*

[3] These included: (1) Agreement Between the Government of the Federal Republic of Germany and the Government of the German Democratic Republic on Transit Traffic of Civilian Persons and Goods Between the Federal Republic of Germany and Berlin (West) of December 17, 1971; (2) Arrangement Between the *Senat* of [West] Berlin and the Government of the German Democratic Republic Concerning the Facilitation and Improvement of Travel and Visitor Traffic of December 20, 1971; (3) Arrangement Between the *Senate* of [West] Berlin and the Government of the German Democratic Republic on the Regulation of the Enclaves Question by Exchange of Territory of December 20, 1971; and (4) Point 6 and 7 of the Protocol on Negotiations Between a Delegation of the Ministry of Posts and Telecommunications of the Federal Republic of Germany and a Delegation of the Ministry of Posts and Telecommunications of the German Democratic Republic of September 30, 1971. All *ante.*

3. The Quadripartite Agreement and the consequent agreements and arrangements of the competent German authorities referred to in this Protocol settle important issues examined in the course of the negotiations and shall remain in force together.

4. In the event of a difficulty in the application of the Quadripartite Agreement or any of the above-mentioned agreements or arrangements which any of the four Governments consider serious, or in the event of non-implementation of any part thereof, that Government will have the right to draw the attention of the other three Governments to the provisions of the Quadripartite Agreement and this Protocol and to conduct the requisite quadripartite consultations in order to ensure the observance of the commitments undertaken and to bring the situation into conformity with the Quadripartite Agreement and this Protocol.

5. This Protocol enters into force on the date of signature.

Done at the building formerly occupied by the Allied Control Council in the American Sector of Berlin this third day of June 1972, in four originals each in the English, French and Russian languages, all texts being equally authentic.

For the Government of the French Republic
MAURICE SCHUMANN

For the Government of the Union of Soviet Socialist Republics
A. GROMYKO

For the Government of the United Kingdom of Great Britain and Northern Ireland
DOUGLAS-HOME

For the Government of the United States of America
WILLIAM ROGERS

Appendix B. Tripartite Agreements

B1. Basic Principles for Merger of the Three Western German Zones of Occupation and Creation of an Allied High Commission, Signed at Washington, April 8, 1949

B2. Occupation Statute Defining the Powers To Be Retained by the Occupation Authorities, Signed by the Three Western Foreign Ministers, April 8, 1949

B3. Convention on Relations Between the Three Powers and the Federal Republic of Germany, May 26, 1952, As Amended by Schedule I of the Protocol on Termination of the Occupation Regime in Germany, Signed at Paris, October 23, 1954

B4. Convention on the Settlement of Matters Arising Out of the War and Occupation, May 26, 1952, As Amended by Schedule IV of the Protocol on Termination of the Occupation Regime in Germany, Signed at Paris, October 23, 1954

B5. Declaration on Berlin Governing Relations Between the Allied (Western) Kommandatura and Berlin, Issued by the Three Western Commandants, May 26, 1952

B6. Convention on the Presence of Foreign Forces in the Federal Republic of Germany, October 23, 1954

Document B1

*Basic Principles for Merger of the Three Western German Zones of
Occupation and Creation of an Allied High Commission, Signed at
Washington, April 8, 1949* [1]

AGREEMENT AS TO TRIPARTITE CONTROLS

The Governments of the United Kingdom, France and the
United States agree to enter into a trizonal fusion agreement prior
to the entry into effect of the Occupation Statute.[2] The representatives of the three occupying powers will make the necessary arrangements to establish tripartite control machinery for the western zones of Germany, which will become effective at the time of
the establishment of a provisional German government. The following provisions agreed by the Governments of the United Kingdom,
France and the United States shall form the basis of these arrangements:

1. An Allied High Commission composed of one High Commissioner of each occupying power or his representative shall be the
supreme Allied agency of control.

2. The nature and extent of controls exercised by the Allied High
Commission shall be in harmony with the Occupation Statute and
international agreements.

3. In order to permit the German Federal Republic to exercise
increased responsibilities over domestic affairs and to reduce the
burden of occupation costs, staff personnel shall be kept to a minimum.

4. In the exercise of the powers reserved to the Occupation Authorities to approve amendments to the Federal Constitution, the
decisions of the Allied High Commission shall require unanimous
agreement.

5. In cases in which the exercise of, or failure to exercise, the
powers reserved under paragraph 5 [2] (g) of the Occupation Statute would increase the need for assistance from United States Government appropriated funds, there shall be a system of weighted
voting. Under such system the representatives of the Occupation
Authorities will have a voting strength proportionate to the funds
made available to Germany by their respective governments. This
provision shall not, however, reduce the present United States predominant voice in JEIA and JFEA while these organizations, or
any successor organization to them, continue in existence and are
charged with the performance of any of their present functions. No
action taken hereunder shall be contrary to any inter-governmental agreement among the signatories or to the principles of non-discrimination.

6. On all other matters action shall be by majority vote.

7. (a) If a majority decision alters or modifies any intergovern-
mental agreement which relates to any of the subjects listed in
paragraph 5 [2] (a) and 5 [2] (b) of the Occupation Statute, any dis-
senting High Commissioner may appeal to his Government. This

appeal shall serve to suspend the decision pending agreement between the three governments.

(b) If a High Commissioner considers that a majority decision conflicts with any inter-governmental agreement which relates to any of the subjects in paragraph 5 [2] (a) and 5 [2] (b) of the Occupation Statute or with the fundamental principles for the conduct of Germany's external relations or with matters essential to the security, prestige, and requirements of the occupying forces, he may appeal to his Government. Such an appeal shall serve to suspend action for 30 days, and thereafter unless two of the Governments indicate that the grounds do not justify further suspension.

(c) If such appeal is from an action of the Allied High Commission either declining to disapprove or deciding to disapprove German legislation, such legislation shall be provisionally disapproved for the duration of the appeal period.

8. A High Commissioner who considers that a decision made by less than unanimous vote involving any other matter reserved by the Occupation Statute is not in conformity with basic tripartite policies regarding Germany or that a Land constitution, or an amendment thereto, violates the Basic Law, may appeal to his Government. An appeal in this case shall serve to suspend action for a period not to exceed twenty-one days from the date of the decision unless all three governments agree otherwise. If such appeal is from an action of the Allied High Commission either declining to disapprove or deciding to disapprove German legislation, such legislation shall be provisionally disapproved for the duration of the appeal period.

9. All powers of the Allied High Commission shall be uniformly exercised in accordance with tripartite policies and directives. To this end in each Land the Allied High Commission shall be represented by a single Land Commissioner who shall be solely responsible to it for all tripartite affairs. In each Land the Land Commissioner shall be a national of the Allied Power in whose zone the Land is situated. Outside his own zone each High Commissioner will delegate an observer to each of the Land Commissioners for purposes of consultation and information. Nothing in this paragraph shall be construed to limit the functions of bodies established pursuant to inter-governmental agreement.

10. To the greatest extent possible, all directives and other instruments of control shall be addressed to the federal and/or Land authorities.

11. The Trizonal Fusion Agreement will continue in force until altered by agreement among the governments.

Document B2

Occupation Statute Defining the Powers To Be Retained by the Occupation Authorities, Signed by the Three Western Foreign Ministers, April 8, 1949 [1]

In the exercise of the supreme authority which is retained by the Governments of France, the United States and the United Kingdom,

---

[1] *Basic Law and Occupation Statute,* pp. 5-7. The Occupation Statute entered into force on September 21, 1949.

We, General PIERRE KOENIG, Military Governor and Commander-in-Chief of the French Zone of Germany,

General LUCIUS D. CLAY, Military Governor and Commander-in-Chief of the United States Zone of Germany, and

General Sir BRIAN HUBERT ROBERTSON, Military Governor and Commander-in-Chief of the British Zone of Germany,

DO HEREBY JOINTLY PROCLAIM THE FOLLOWING OCCUPATION STATUTE:

1. During the period in which it is necessary that the occupation continue, the Governments of France, the United States and the United Kingdom desire and intend that the German people shall enjoy self-government to the maximum possible degree consistent with such occupation. The Federal state and the participating Laender shall have, subject only to the limitations in this instrument, full legislative, executive and judicial powers in accordance with the Basic Law and with their respective constitutions.

2. In order to ensure the accomplishment of the basic purposes of the occupation, powers in the following fields are specifically reserved, including the right to request and verify information and statistics needed by the Occupation Authorities:

(a) Disarmament and demilitarization, including related fields of scientific research, prohibitions and restrictions on industry, and civil aviation;

(b) Controls in regard to the Ruhr, restitution, reparations, decartelization, deconcentration, non-discrimination in trade matters, foreign interests in Germany and claims against Germany;

(c) Foreign affairs, including international agreements made by or on behalf of Germany;

(d) Displaced persons and the admission of refugees;

(e) Protection, prestige, and security of Allied Forces, dependents, employees and representatives, their immunities and satisfaction of occupation costs and of their other requirements;

(f) Respect for the Basic Law and the Land Constitutions;

(g) Control over foreign trade and exchange;

(h) Control over internal action, only to the minimum extent necessary to ensure use of funds, food and other supplies in such manner as to reduce to a minimum the need for external assistance to Germany;

(i) Control of the care and treatment in German prisons of persons charged before or sentenced by the courts or tribunals of the Occupying Powers or Occupation Authorities; over the carrying out of sentences imposed on them; and over questions of amnesty, pardon or release in reaction to them.

3. It is the hope and expectation of the Governments of France, the United States, and the United Kingdom that the Occupation Authorities will not have occasion to take action in fields other than those specifically reserved above. The Occupation Authorities, however, reserve the right, acting under instructions of their Governments, to resume, in whole or in part, the exercise of full au-

thority if they consider that to do so is essential to security or to preserve democratic government in Germany or in pursuance of the international obligations of their Governments. Before so doing they will formally advise the appropriate German authorities of their decision and the reasons therefor.

4. The German Federal government and the governments of the Laender shall have the power, after due notification to the Occupation Authorities, to legislate and act in the fields reserved to these authorities, except as the Occupation Authorities otherwise specifically direct, or as such legislation or action would be inconsistent with decisions or actions taken by the Occupation Authorities themselves.

5. Any amendment of the Basic Law will require the express approval of the Occupation Authorities before becoming effective. Land constitutions, amendments thereof, all other legislation, and any agreements made between the Federal state and foreign governments, will become effective twenty-one days after official receipt by the Occupation Authorities unless previously disapproved by them, provisionally or finally. The Occupation Authorities will not disapprove legislation unless in their opinion it is inconsistent with the Basic Law, a Land constitution, legislation or other directives of the Occupation Authorities themselves or the provisions of this instrument or unless it constitutes a grave threat to the basic purposes of the occupation.

6. Subject only to the requirements of their security, the Occupation Authorities guarantee that all agencies of the occupation will respect the civil rights of every person to be protected against arbitrary arrest, search or seizure; to be represented by counsel; to be admitted to bail as circumstances warrant; to communicate with relatives; and to have a fair and prompt trial.

7. Legislation of the Occupation Authorities enacted before the effective date of the Basic Law shall remain in force until repealed or amended by the Occupation Authorities in accordance with the following provisions:

(a) Legislation inconsistent with the foregoing will be repealed or amended to make it consistent herewith;
(b) Legislation based upon the reserved powers, referred to in para 2 above, will be codified;
(c) Legislation not referred to in (a) and (b) will be repealed by the Occupation Authorities on request from appropriate German authorities.

8. Any action shall be deemed to be the act of the Occupation Authorities under the powers herein reserved, and effective as such under this instrument, when taken or evidenced in any matter provided by any agreement between them. The Occupation Authorities may in their discretion effectuate their decisions either directly or through instructions to the appropriate German authorities.

9. After 12 months and in any event within 18 months of the effective date of this instrument the Occupying Powers will undertake a review of its provisions in the light of experience with its operation and with a view to extending the jurisdiction of the German authorities in the legislative, executive and judicial fields.

Document B3

Convention on Relations Between the Three Powers and the Federal Republic of Germany, May 26, 1952, As Amended by Schedule I of the Protocol on Termination of the Occupation Regime in Germany, Signed at Paris, October 23, 1954 [1]

THE UNITED STATES OF AMERICA,
THE UNITED KINGDOM OF GREAT BRITAIN AND NORTHERN IRELAND
THE FRENCH REPUBLIC AND
THE FEDERAL REPUBLIC OF GERMANY

HAVE entered into the following Convention setting forth the basis for their new relationship:

ARTICLE 1

1. On the entry into force of the present Convention the United States of America, the United Kingdom of Great Britain and Northern Ireland and the French Republic (hereinafter and in the related Conventions sometimes referred to as "the Three Powers") will terminate the Occupation regime in the Federal Republic, revoke the Occupation Statute [2] and abolish the Allied High Commission and the Offices of the Land Commissioners in the Federal Republic. [3]

2. The Federal Republic shall have accordingly the full authority of a sovereign state over its internal and external affairs.

ARTICLE 2

In view of the international situation, which has so far prevented the reunification of Germany and the conclusion of a peace settlement, the Three Powers retain the rights and the responsibilities, heretofore exercised or held by them, relating to Berlin and to Germany as a whole, including the reunification of Germany and a peace settlement. The rights and responsibilities retained by the Three Powers relating to the stationing of armed forces in Germany and the protection of their security are dealt with in Articles 4 and 5 of the present Convention.

ARTICLE 3

1. The Federal Republic agrees to conduct its policy in accordance with the principles set forth in the Charter of the United Nations and with the aims defined in the Statute of the Council of Europe. [4]

---

[1] *The Bonn Agreements of 1952 as Amended by the Paris Protocol of 1954* (S. Doc. 11, 84th Cong., 1st sess.), pp. 129–140; this convention entered into force on May 5, 1955. For the 1952 text of this convention, see *Convention on Relations With the Federal Republic of Germany and a Protocol to the North Atlantic Treaty*, pp. 9–22.

[2] *Ante* under date of April 8, 1949.

[3] The Allied High Commission and the Offices of the Land Commissioners were established in the Charter of the Allied High Commission, June 20, 1949; for extracts from the Charter. see *ante.*

[4] Statute of May 5, 1949, as amended; *American Foreign Policy, 1950–1955,* pp. 1001–1012.

2. The Federal Republic affirms its intention to associate itself fully with the community of free nations through membership in international organizations contributing to the common aims of the free world. The Three Powers will support applications for such membership by the Federal Republic at appropriate times.

3. In their negotiations with States with which the Federal Republic maintains no relations, the Three Powers will consult with the Federal Republic in respect of matters directly involving its political interests.

4. At the request of the Federal Government, the Three Powers will arrange to represent the interests of the Federal Republic in relations with other States and in certain international organizations or conferences, whenever the Federal Republic is not in a position to do so itself.

ARTICLE 4

1. Pending the entry into force of the arrangements for the German Defence Contribution,[5] the Three Powers retain the rights, heretofore exercised or held by them, relating to the stationing of armed forces in the Federal Republic. The mission of these forces will be the defence of the free world, of which Berlin and the Federal Republic form part. Subject to the provisions of paragraph 2 of Article 5 of the present Convention, the rights and obligations of these forces shall be governed by the Convention on the Rights and Obligations of Foreign Forces and their Members in the Federal Republic of Germany [6] (hereinafter referred to as "the Forces Convention") referred to in paragraph 1 of Article 8 of the present Convention.

2. The rights of the Three Powers, heretofore exercised or held by them, which relate to the stationing of armed forces in Germany and which are retained, are not affected by the provisions of this Article insofar as they are required for the exercise of the rights referred to in the first sentence of Article 2 of the present Convention. The Federal Republic agrees that, from the entry into force of the arrangements for the German Defence Contribution, forces of the same nationality and effective strength as at that time may be stationed in the Federal Republic. In view of the status of the Federal Republic as defined in Article 1, paragraph 2 of the present Convention and in view of the fact that the Three Powers do not desire to exercise their rights regarding the stationing of armed forces in the Federal Republic, insofar as it is concerned, except in full accord with the Federal Republic, a separate Convention deals with this matter.[7]

---

[5] See the Protocol modifying and completing the Brussels Treaty; *ibid.*, pp. 972-976.

[6] Convention of May 26, 1952, as amended by protocol of October 23, 1954; *ibid.*, pp. 498-539.

[7] For the text of the Convention of October 23, 1954, on the presence of foreign forces in the German Federal Republic, see *ibid.*, pp. 610-612.

ARTICLE 5

1. Pending the entry into force of the arrangements for the German Defence Contribution, the following provisions shall be applicable to the forces stationed in the Federal Republic:

(a) The Three Powers will consult with the Federal Republic, insofar as the military situation permits, with regard to all questions concerning the stationing of these forces. The Federal Republic will, according to the present Convention and the related Conventions, co-operate, within the framework of its Basic Law,[8] to facilitate the mission of these forces;

(b) The Three Powers will obtain the consent of the Federal Republic before bringing into the Federal territory, as part of their forces, contingents of the armed forces of any nation not now providing such contingents. Such contingents may nevertheless be brought into the Federal territory without the consent of the Federal Republic in the event of external attack or imminent threat of such attack, but, after the elimination of the danger, may only remain with its consent.

2. The rights of the Three Powers, heretofore held or exercised by them, which relate to the protection of the security of armed forces stationed in the Federal Republic and which are temporarily retained, shall lapse when the appropriate German authorities have obtained similar powers under German legislation enabling them to take effective action to protect the security of those forces, including the ability to deal with a serious disturbance of public security and order. To the extent that such rights continue to be exercisable they shall be exercised only after consultation, insofar as the military situation does not preclude such consultation, with the Federal Government and with its agreement that the circumstances require such exercise. In all other respects the protection of the security of those forces shall be governed by the Forces Convention or by the provisions of the Agreement which replaces it and, except as otherwise provided in any applicable agreement, by German law.

ARTICLE 6

1. The Three Powers will consult with the Federal Republic in regard to the exercise of their rights relating to Berlin.
2. The Federal Republic, on its part, will co-operate with the Three Powers in order to facilitate the discharge of their responsibilities with regard to Berlin.

ARTICLE 7

1. The Signatory States are agreed that an essential aim of their common policy is a peace settlement for the whole of Germany, freely negotiated between Germany and her former enemies, which should lay the foundation for a lasting peace. They further agree

that the final determination of the boundaries of Germany must await such settlement.

2. Pending the peace settlement, the Signatory States will cooperate to achieve, by peaceful means, their common aim of a reunified Germany enjoying a liberal-democratic constitution, like that of the Federal Republic, and integrated within the European community.

3. [Deleted.]

4. The Three Powers will consult with the Federal Republic on all matters involving the exercise of their rights relating to Germany as a whole.

ARTICLE 8

1. (a) The Signatory States have concluded the following related Conventions:

> Convention on the Rights and Obligations of Foreign Forces and their Members in the Federal Republic of Germany;[9]
> Finance Convention;[10]
> Convention on the Settlement of Matters Arising out of the War and the Occupation.[11]

(b) The Convention on the Rights and Obligations of Foreign Forces and their Members in the Federal Republic of Germany and the Agreement on Tax Treatment of the Forces and their Members signed at Bonn on 26 May 1952, as amended by the Protocol signed at Bonn on 26 July 1952 [12] shall remain in force until the entry into force of new arrangements setting forth the rights and obligations of the forces of the Three Powers and other States having forces in the territory of the Federal Republic. The new arrangements will be based on the Agreement Between the Parties to the North Atlantic Treaty Regarding the Status of their Forces, signed at London on 19 June 1951,[13] supplemented by such provisions as are necessary in view of the special conditions existing in regard to the forces stationed in the Federal Republic.

(c) The Finance Convention shall remain in force until the entry into force of the new arrangements negotiated in pursuance of paragraph 4 of Article 4 of that Convention with other member Governments of the North Atlantic Treaty Organization who have forces stationed in the Federal territory.

2. During the transitional period provided for in paragraph 4 of Article 6 of Chapter One of the Convention on the Settlement of Matters Arising out of the War and the Occupation, the rights of the three Signatory States referred to in that paragraph shall be retained.

ARTICLE 9

1. There shall be established an Arbitration Tribunal which shall function in accordance with the provisions of the annexed Charter.[14]

2. The Arbitration Tribunal shall have exclusive jurisdiction over all disputes arising between the Three Powers and the Federal Republic under the provisions of the present Convention or the annexed Charter or any of the related Conventions which the parties are not able to settle by negotiation or by other means agreed between all the Signatory States, except as otherwise provided by paragraph 3 of this Article or in the annexed Charter or in the related Conventions.

3. Any dispute involving the rights of the Three Powers referred to in Article 2, the first two sentences of paragraph 1 of Article 4, the first sentence of paragraph 2 of Article 4 and the first two sentences of paragraph 2 of Article 5, or action taken thereunder shall not be subject to the jurisdiction of the Arbitration Tribunal or of any other tribunal or court.

ARTICLE 10

The Signatory States will review the terms of the present Convention and the related Conventions

(a) upon request of any one of them, in the event of the reunification of Germany, or an international understanding being reached with the participation or consent of the States parties to the present Convention on steps towards bringing about the reunification of Germany, or the creation of a European Federation; or

(b) in any situation which all of the Signatory States recognize has resulted from a change of a fundamental character in the conditions prevailing at the time of the entry into force of the present Convention.

In either case they will, by mutual agreement, modify the present Convention and the related Conventions to the extent made necessary or advisable by the fundamental change in the situation.

ARTICLE 11

1. [Deleted.]
2. [Deleted.]
3. The present Convention and the related Conventions shall be deposited in the Archives of the Government of the Federal Republic of Germany, which will furnish each Signatory State with certi-

fied copies thereof and notify each such State of the date of the entry into force of the present Convention [15] and the related Conventions.

IN FAITH WHEREOF the undersigned representatives duly authorized thereto by their respective Governments have signed the present Convention.

Done at BONN this twenty-sixth day of May, 1952, in three texts, in the English, French and German languages, all being equally authentic.

For the United States of America
    signed: DEAN ACHESON
For the United Kingdom of Great Britain and Northern Ireland
    signed: ANTHONY EDEN
For the French Republic
    signed: ROBERT SCHUMAN
For the Federal Republic of Germany
    signed: ADENAUER

---

[15] The convention entered into force simultaneously with the Protocol on the Termination of the Occupation Regime, May 5, 1955, in accordance with article 1 of the Protocol.

Document B4

Convention on the Settlement of Matters Arising Out of the War and Occupation, May 26, 1952, As Amended by Schedule IV of the Protocol on Termination of the Occupation Regime in Germany, Signed at Paris, October 23, 1954 [1]

[Extracts]

THE UNITED STATES OF AMERICA,
THE UNITED KINGDOM OF GREAT BRITAIN AND NORTHERN IRE-
LAND,
THE FRENCH REPUBLIC
   and
THE FEDERAL REPUBLIC OF GERMANY,
Agree as follows:

.   .   .   .

CHAPTER TWELVE—CIVIL AVIATION

.   .   .   .

ARTICLE 5

1. In the exercise of their responsibilities with respect to Berlin, the Three Powers will continue to regulate all air traffic to and from the Berlin air corridors established by the Allied Control Authority. The Federal Republic undertakes to facilitate and assist such traffic in every way on a basis no less favourable than that enjoyed on the entry into force of the present Convention; it undertakes to facilitate and assist unlimited and unimpeded passage through its air space for aircraft of the Three Powers en route to and from Berlin. The Federal Republic agrees to permit any necessary technical stops by such aircraft and further agrees that such aircraft may carry passengers, cargo and mail between places outside the Federal Republic and Berlin and between the Federal Republic and Berlin.

2. Nothing in this Article shall confer or affect any cabotage privileges within the Federal territory.

ARTICLE 6

In the exercise of their responsibilities relating to Germany as a whole, the Three Powers will continue to exercise control with respect to aircraft of the Union of Soviet Socialist Republics utilizing the air space of the Federal Republic.

    •   •   •   •   •   •   •

Document B5

Declaration on Berlin Governing Relations Between the Allied (Western) Kommandatura and Berlin, Issued by the Three Western Commandants, May 26, 1952 [1]

Taking into consideration the new relations established between France, the United Kingdom of Great Britain and Northern Ire-

---

[1] *American Foreign Policy, 1950–1955,* pp. 1740-1742. This Declaration entered into force on May 5, 1955.

land, the United States of America, and the Federal Republic of
Germany and wishing to grant the Berlin authorities the maximum liberty compatible with the special situation of Berlin,
the Allied Kommandatura makes this declaration:

I

Berlin shall exercise all its rights, powers and responsibilities set
forth in its Constitution as adopted in 1950 subject only to the reservations made by the Allied Kommandatura on 29th August
1950,[2] and to the provisions hereinafter.

II

The Allied authorities retain the right to take, if they deem it
necessary, such measures as may be required to fulfill their international obligations, to ensure public order and to maintain the
status and security of Berlin and its economy, trade and communications.

III

The Allied authorities will normally exercise powers only in the
following fields:

(a) Security, interests and immunities of the Allied Forces,
including their representatives, dependents and non-German
employees. German employees of the Allied Forces enjoy immunity from German jurisdiction only in matters arising out
of or in the course of performance of duties or services with
the Allied Forces;

(b) Disarmament and demilitarisation, including related
fields of scientific research, civil aviation, and prohibitions and
restrictions on industry in relation to the foregoing;

(c) Relations of Berlin with authorities abroad. However, the
Allied Kommandatura will permit the Berlin authorities to
assure the representation abroad of the interests of Berlin and
of its inhabitants by suitable arrangements;

(d) Satisfaction of occupation costs. These costs will be fixed
after consultation with the appropriate German authorities
and at the lowest level consistent with maintaining the security of Berlin and of the Allied Forces located there;

(e) Authority over the Berlin police to the extent necessary
to ensure the security of Berlin.

IV

The Allied Kommandatura will not, subject to Articles I and II of
this Declaration, raise any objection to the adoption by Berlin
under an appropriate procedure authorised by the Allied Kommandatura of the same legislation as that of the Federal Republic, in
particular regarding currency, credit and foreign exchange, nationality, passports, emigration and immigration, extradition, the unifi-

cation of the customs and trade area, trade and navigation agreements, freedom of movement of goods, and foreign trade and payments arrangements.

V

In the following fields:

(a) restitution, reparations, decartelisation, deconcentration, foreign interests in Berlin, claims against Berlin or its inhabitants,

(b) displaced persons and the admission of refugees,

(c) control of the care and treatment in German prisons of persons charged before or sentenced by Allied courts or tribunals; over the carrying out of sentences imposed on them and over questions of amnesty, pardon or release in relation to them,

the Allied authorities will in future only intervene to an extent consistent with, or if the Berlin authorities act inconsistently with, the principles which form the basis of the new relations between France, the United Kingdom and the United States on the one part and the Federal Republic of Germany on the other, or with the Allied legislation in force in Berlin.

VI

All legislation of the Allied authorities will remain in force until repealed, amended or deprived of effect.

The Allied authorities will repeal, amend or deprive of effect any legislation which they deem no longer appropriate in the light of this declaration.

Legislation of the Allied authorities may also be repealed or amended by Berlin legislation; but such repeal or amendment shall require the approval of the Allied authorities before coming into force.

VII

Berlin legislation shall come into force in accordance with the provisions of the Berlin Constitution. In cases of inconsistency with Allied legislation, or with other measures of the Allied authorities, or with the rights of the Allied authorities under this declaration, Berlin legislation will be subject to repeal or annulment by the Allied Kommandatura.

VIII

In order to enable them to fulfill their obligations under this declaration, the Allied authorities shall have the right to request and obtain such information and statistics as they deem necessary.

IX

The Allied Kommandatura will modify the provisions of this declaration as the situation in Berlin permits.

X

Upon the effective date of this declaration the Statement of Principles Governing the Relationship between the Allied Kommandatura and Greater Berlin of 14th May, 1949, as modified by the First Instrument of Revision, dated 7th March, 1951,[3] will be repealed.

Document B6

19. CONVENTION ON THE PRESENCE OF FOREIGN FORCES IN THE FEDERAL REPUBLIC OF GERMANY, OCTOBER 23, 1954 [1]

In view of the present international situation and the need to ensure the defence of the free world which require the continuing presence of foreign forces in the Federal Republic of Germany, the United States of America, the United Kingdom of Great Britain and Northern Ireland, the French Republic and the Federal Republic of Germany agree as follows:

ARTICLE 1

1. From the entry into force of the arrangements for the German Defence Contribution,[2] forces of the same nationality and effective strength as at that time may be stationed in the Federal Republic.

2. The effective strength of the forces stationed in the Federal Republic pursuant to paragraph 1 of this Article may at any time be increased with the consent of the Government of the Federal Republic of Germany.

3. Additional forces of the States parties to the present Convention may enter and remain in the Federal territory with the consent of the Government of the Federal Republic of Germany for training purposes in accordance with the procedures applicable to forces assigned to the Supreme Allied Commander, Europe, provided that such forces do not remain there for more than thirty days at any one time.

4. The Federal Republic grants to the French, the United Kingdom and the United States forces the right to enter, pass through and depart from the territory of the Federal Republic in transit to or from Austria (so long as their forces continue to be stationed there) or any country Member of the North Atlantic Treaty Organization, on the same basis as is usual between Parties to the North Atlantic Treaty or as may be agreed with effect for all Member States by the North Atlantic Council.

---

[1] S. Execs. L and M, 83d Cong., 2d sess., pp. 89–90. Approved by the President Apr. 7, 1955; entered into force May 6, 1955.

[2] See the Protocols of Oct 23, 1954, to the North Atlantic Treaty and the Brussels Treaty; *infra*, pp. 871–873 and 972–989. See also the Final Act of the London Conference, Oct. 3, 1954, *infra*, pp. 1474–1491.

ARTICLE 2

The present Convention shall be open to accession by any State not a Signatory, which had forces stationed in the Federal territory on the date of the signature of the Protocol on the Termination of the Occupation Regime in the Federal Republic of Germany signed at Paris on 23 October 1954.[1] Any such State, desiring to accede to the present Convention, may deposit with the Government of the Federal Republic an Instrument of Accession.[2]

ARTICLE 3

1. The present Convention shall expire with the conclusion of a German peace settlement or if at an earlier time the Signatory States agree that the development of the international situation justifies new arrangements.
2. The Signatory States will review the terms of the present Convention at the same time and subject to the same conditions as provided for in Article 10 of the Convention on Relations between the Three Powers and the Federal Republic of Germany.[3]

ARTICLE 4

1. The present Convention shall be ratified or approved by the Signatory States and Instruments of Ratification or Approval shall be deposited by them with the Government of the Federal Republic of Germany which shall notify each Signatory State of the deposit of each Instrument of Ratification or Approval. The present Convention shall enter into force when all the Signatory States have made such deposit and the Instrument of Accession of the Federal Republic of Germany to the North Atlantic Treaty has been deposited with the Government of the United States of America.
2. It shall also enter into force on that date as to any acceding State which has previously deposited an Instrument of Accession in accordance with Article 2 of the present Convention and, as to any other acceding State, on the date of the deposit by it of such an Instrument.
3. The present Convention shall be deposited in the Archives of the Government of the Federal Republic of Germany, which will furnish each State party to the present Convention with certified copies thereof and of the Instruments of Accession deposited in accordance with

Article 2 and will notify each State of the date of the deposit of any Instrument of Accession.

IN FAITH WHEREOF the undersigned Representatives duly authorized thereto have signed the present Convention.

Done at Paris this 23rd day of October, 1954, in three texts, in the English, French and German languages, all being equally authentic.

---

[1] *Supra*, pp. 483–485.
[2] As of Dec. 31, 1955, the following states had deposited, on the dates indicated, their instruments of accession to this convention: Belgium, Apr. 22, 1955; the Netherlands, Apr. 30, 1955; Canada, May 3, 1955; Denmark and Luxembourg, May 4, 1955.
[3] *Supra*, p. 490.

Appendix C. NATO and Multilateral Agreements

C1. Final Act of the Nine-Power Conference, London, October 3, 1954

C2. Protocol to the North Atlantic Treaty on the Accession of the Federal Republic of Germany, Signed at Paris, October 23, 1954

C3. Protocol No. II on Forces of Western European Union, October 23, 1954

C4. Draft Resolution to Implement Section IV of the Final Act of the London Conference, Paris, October 19, 1954

C5. Final Act of the Conference on Security and Co-operation in Europe, Helsinki, August 1, 1975

PAUL B. STARES

Document C1

Final Act of the Nine-Power Conference, London, October 3, 1954 [1]

[Extracts]

The Conference of the Nine Powers, Belgium, Canada, France, German Federal Republic, Italy, Luxembourg, Netherlands, United Kingdom of Great Britain and Northern Ireland and United States met in London from Tuesday September Twenty-eighth to Sunday October Third. It dealt with the most important issues facing the Western world, security and European integration within the framework of a developing Atlantic community dedicated to peace

---

[1] *London and Paris Agreements, September–October 1954* (Department of State publication 5659), pp. 9–29.

and freedom. In this connexion the Conference considered how to assure the full association of the German Federal Republic with the West and the German defence contribution.

Belgium was represented by His Excellency Monsieur P-H Spaak.

Canada was represented by the Honourable L. B. Pearson.

France was represented by His Excellency Monsieur P. Mendès-France.

The Federal Republic of Germany was represented by His Excellency Dr. K. Adenauer.

Italy was represented by His Excellency Professor G. Martino.

Luxembourg was represented by His Excellency Monsieur J. Bech.

The Netherlands was represented by His Excellency J. W. Beyen.

The United Kingdom of Great Britain and Northern Ireland was represented by Rt. Hon. A. Eden, M.C., M.P.

The United States of America was represented by the Honourable J.F. Dulles.

All the decisions of the Conference formed part of one general settlement which is, directly or indirectly, of concern to all the NATO powers and which will therefore be submitted to the North Atlantic Council for information or decision.

I. GERMANY

The Governments of France, the United Kingdom and the United States declare that their policy is to end the Occupation régime in the Federal Republic as soon as possible, to revoke the Occupation Statute and to abolish the Allied High Commission. The Three Governments will continue to discharge certain responsibilities in Germany arising out of the international situation.

It is intended to conclude, and to bring into force as soon as the necessary parliamentary procedures have been completed, the appropriate instruments for these purposes. General agreement has already been reached on the content of these instruments and representatives of the Four Governments will meet in the very near future to complete the final texts. The agreed arrangements may be put into effect either before or simultaneously with the arrangements for the German defense contribution.

As these arrangements will take a little time to complete, the Three Governments have in the meantime issued the following Declaration of Intent:

Recognising that a great country can no longer be deprived of the rights properly belonging to a free and democratic people; and

Desiring to associate the Federal Republic of Germany on a footing of equality with their efforts for peace and security.

The Governments of France, the United Kingdom, the United States of America desire to end the Occupation régime as soon as possible.

The fulfillment of this policy calls for the settlement of problems of detail in order to liquidate the past and to prepare for the future, and requires the completion of appropriate Parliamentary procedures.

In the meantime, the Three Governments are instructing their High Commissioners to act forthwith in accordance with the spirit of the above policy. In particular, the High Commissioners will not use the powers which are to be relinquished unless in agreement with the Federal Government, except in the fields of disarmament and demilitarisation and in cases where the Federal Government has not been able for legal reasons to take the action or assume the obligations contemplated in the agreed arrangement.

II. BRUSSELS TREATY [2]

The Brussels Treaty will be strengthened and extended to make it a more effective focus of European integration.

For this purpose the following arrangements have been agreed upon:

(a) The German Federal Republic and Italy will be invited to accede to the Treaty, suitably modified to emphasise the objective of European unity, and they have declared themselves ready to do so. The system of mutual automatic assistance in case of attack will thus be extended to the German Federal Republic and Italy.

•   •   •   •   •   •   •

15. The Brussels Treaty Powers have taken note of the following Declaration of the Chancellor of the Federal Republic of Germany and record their agreement with it:

The Federal Chancellor Declares:

That the Federal Republic undertakes not to manufacture in its territory any atomic weapons, chemical weapons or biological weapons as detailed in paragraphs I, II and III of the attached lists;

That it undertakes further not to manufacture in its territory such weapons as those detailed in paragraphs IV, V and VI of the attached list. Any amendment to or cancellation of the substance of paragraphs IV, V and VI can, on the request of the Federal Republic, be carried out by a resolution of the Brussels Council of Ministers by a two-thirds majority, if, in accordance with the needs of the armed forces, a request is made by the competent supreme commander of NATO;

That the Federal Republic agrees to supervision by the competent authority of the Brussels Treaty Organization to ensure that these undertakings are observed.

List Appended to the Declaration by the Federal Chancellor

This list comprises the weapons defined in paragraphs I to VI and the factories earmarked solely for their production. All apparatus, parts, equipment installations, substances and organisms which are used for civilian purposes or for scientific, medical and industrial research in the fields of pure and applied science shall be excluded from this definition.

I. *Atomic weapons*

Text as in Annex II paragraph I to Article 107 of the EDC Treaty [3] with the deletion of (c).

II. *Chemical weapons*

III. *Biological weapons*

IV. *Long distance missiles, guided missiles, magnetic and influence mines*

Texts as in Annex II paragraphs II, III, IV to Article 107 of the EDC Treaty.

V. *Warships, with the exception of smaller ships for defence purposes*

"Warships with the exception of smaller ships for defence purposes" are:

(a) Warships of more than 3,000 tons displacement.

(b) Submarines of more than 350 tons displacement.

(c) All warships which are driven by means other than steam, diesel or petrol engines or by gas turbines or by jet engines.

VI. *Bomber aircraft for strategic purposes*

The closest possible co-operation with NATO shall be established in all fields.

• • • • • • •

V. DECLARATION BY THE GERMAN FEDERAL GOVERNMENT AND JOINT DECLARATION BY THE GOVERNMENTS OF FRANCE, UNITED KINGDOM, AND UNITED STATES OF AMERICA

The following declarations were recorded at the Conference by the German Federal Chancellor and by the Foreign Ministers of France, United Kingdom and United States of America

Declaration by German Federal Republic

The German Federal Republic has agreed to conduct its policy in accordance with principles of the Charter of the United Nations and accepts the obligations set forth in Article 2 of the Charter.

Upon her accession to the North Atlantic Treaty and the Brussels Treaty, the German Federal Republic declares that she will refrain from any action inconsistent with the strictly defensive character of the two treaties. In particular the German Federal Republic undertakes never to have recourse to force to achieve the reunification of Germany or the modification of the present boundaries of the German Federal Republic, and to resolve by peaceful means any disputes which may arise between the Federal Republic and other States.

Declaration by the Governments of United States of America, United Kingdom and France

The Governments of the United States of America, the United Kingdom of Great Britain and Northern Ireland and the French Republic.

Being resolved to devote their efforts to the strengthening of peace in accordance with the Charter of the United Nations and in particular with the obligations set forth in Article 2 of the Charter

(i) to settle their international disputes by peaceful means in such a manner that international peace and security and justice are not endangered;

(ii) to refrain in their international relations from the threat or use of force against the territorial integrity or political independence of any State, or in any other manner inconsistent with the purposes of the United Nations;

(iii) to give the United Nations every assistance in any action it takes in accordance with the Charter, and to refrain from giving assistance to any State against which the United Nations take preventive or enforcement action;

(iv) to ensure that States which are not Members of the United Nations act in accordance with the principles of the Charter so far as may be necessary for the maintenance of international peace and security.

Having regard to the purely defensive character of the Atlantic Alliance which is manifest in the North Atlantic Treaty, wherein they reaffirm their faith in the purposes and principles of the Charter of the United Nations and their desire to live in peace with all peoples and all Governments, and undertake to settle their international disputes by peaceful means in accordance with the principles of the Charter and to refrain, in accordance with those principles, from the threat or use in [of] force in their international relations,

Take note that the German Federal Republic has by a Declaration dated October 3rd accepted the obligations set forth in Article 2 of the Charter of the United Nations and has undertaken never to have recourse to force to achieve the reunification of Germany or the modification of the present boundaries of the German Federal Republic, and to resolve by peaceful means any disputes which may arise between the Federal Republic and other states:

DECLARE THAT

1. They consider the Government of the Federal Republic as the only German Government freely and legitimately constituted and therefore entitled to speak for Germany as the representative of the German people in international affairs.

2. In their relations with the Federal Republic they will follow the principles set out in Article 2 of the United Nations Charter.

3. A peace settlement for the whole of Germany, freely negotiated between Germany and her former enemies, which should lay the foundation of a lasting peace, remains an essential aim of their

policy. The final determination of the boundaries of Germany must await such a settlement.

4. The achievement through peaceful means of a fully free and unified Germany remains a fundamental goal of their policy.

5. The security and welfare of Berlin and the maintenance of the position of the Three Powers there are regarded by the Three Powers as essential elements of the peace of the free world in the present international situation. Accordingly they will maintain armed forces within the territory of Berlin as long as their responsibilities require it. They therefore reaffirm that they will treat any attack against Berlin from any quarter as an attack upon their forces and themselves.

6. They will regard as a threat to their own peace and safety any recourse to force which in violation of the principles of the United Nations Charter threatens the integrity and unity of the Atlantic alliance or its defensive purposes. In the event of any such action, the three Governments, for their part, will consider the offending government as having forfeited its rights to any guarantee and any military assistance provided for in the North Atlantic Treaty and its protocols. They will act in accordance with Article 4 of the North Atlantic Treaty with a view to taking other measures which may be appropriate.

7. They will invite the association of other member States of the North Atlantic Treaty Organisation with this Declaration.

Document C2

Protocol to the North Atlantic Treaty on the Accession of the Federal Republic of Germany, Signed at Paris, October 23, 1954 [1]

The Parties to the North Atlantic Treaty signed at Washington on 4th April, 1949,

Being satisfied that the security of the North Atlantic area will be enhanced by the accession of the Federal Republic of Germany to that Treaty, and

Having noted that the Federal Republic of Germany has by a declaration dated 3rd October, 1954, accepted the obligations set forth in Article 2 of the Charter of the United Nations and has undertaken upon its accession to the North Atlantic Treaty to refrain from any action inconsistent with the strictly defensive character of that Treaty, and

Having further noted that all member governments have associated themselves with the declaration also made on 3rd October, 1954, by the Governments of the United States of America, the United Kingdom of Great Britain and Northern Ireland and the French Republic in connection with the aforesaid declaration of the Federal Republic of Germany,[2]

Agree as follows:

ARTICLE I

Upon the entry into force of the present Protocol, the Government of the United States of America shall on behalf of all the Parties communicate to the Government of the Federal Republic of Germany an invitation to accede to the North Atlantic Treaty. Thereafter the Federal Republic of Germany shall become a Party to that Treaty on the date when it deposits its instruments of accession with the Government of the United States of America in accordance with Article 10 of that Treaty.

ARTICLE II

The present Protocol shall enter into force when (a) each of the Parties to the North Atlantic Treaty has notified to the Government of the United States of America its acceptance thereof, (b) all instruments of ratification of the Protocol Modifying and Completing the Brussels Treaty have been deposited with the Belgian Government, and (c) all instruments of ratification or approval of the Convention on the Presence of Foreign Forces in the Federal Republic of Germany have been deposited with the Government of the Federal Republic of Germany. The Government of the United States of America shall inform the other Parties to the North Atlantic Treaty of the date of the receipt of each notification of acceptance of the present Protocol and of the date of the entry into force of the present Protocol.

ARTICLE III

The present Protocol, of which the English and French texts are equally authentic, shall be deposited in the archives of the Government of the United States of America. Duly certified copies thereof shall be transmitted by that Government to the Governments of the other Parties to the North Atlantic Treaty.

IN WITNESS WHEREOF, the undersigned Representatives, duly authorized thereto by their respective Governments, have signed the present Protocol.

Document C3

PROTOCOL NO. II ON FORCES OF WESTERN EUROPEAN UNION, OCTOBER 23, 1954 [1]

His Majesty the King of the Belgians, the President of the French Republic, President of the French Union, the President of the Federal Republic of Germany, the President of the Italian Republic, Her Royal Highness the Grand Duchess of Luxembourg, Her Majesty the Queen of the Netherlands, and Her Majesty the Queen of the United Kingdom of Great Britain and Northern Ireland and of Her other Realms and Territories, Head of the Commonwealth, Signatories of the Protocol Modifying and Completing the Brussels Treaty,
Having consulted the North Atlantic Council,
Have appointed . . . . . . ,
Have agreed as follows:

Article 1

1. The land and air forces which each of the High Contracting Parties to the present Protocol shall place under the Supreme Allied Commander Europe in peacetime on the mainland of Europe shall not exceed in total strength and number of formations:

    (a) for Belgium, France, the Federal Republic of Germany, Italy and the Netherlands, the maxima laid down for peacetime in the Special Agreement annexed to the Treaty on the Establishment of a European Defence Community signed at Paris, on 27th May, 1952;[2] and
    (b) for the United Kingdom, four divisions and the Second Tactical Air Force;
    (c) for Luxembourg, one regimental combat team.

2. The number of formations mentioned in paragraph 1 may be brought up to date and adapted as necessary to make them suitable for the North Atlantic Treaty Organization, provided that the equivalent fighting capacity and total strengths are not exceeded.
3. The statement of these maxima does not commit any of the High Contracting Parties to build up or maintain forces at these levels, but maintains their right to do so if required.

Article 2

As regards naval forces, the contribution to Nato Commands of each of the High Contracting Parties to the present Protocol shall be determined each year in the course of the Annual Review (which takes into account the recommendations of the Nato military authorities). The naval forces of the Federal Republic of Germany shall consist of the vessels and formations necessary for the defensive

---

[1] *London and Paris Agreements, September–October 1954* (Department of State publication 5659; 1954), pp. 42–44. Entered into force May 6, 1955.
[2] For treaty constituting the European Defense Community, see *infra*, doc. 16. The Special Agreement annexed to the Treaty on the Establishment of a European Defense Community has not been published.

missions assigned to it by the North Atlantic Treaty Organization within the limits laid down in the Special Agreement mentioned in Article 1, or equivalent fighting capacity.

Article 3

If at any time during the Annual Review recommendations are put forward, the effect of which would be to increase the level of forces above the limits specified in Articles 1 and 2, the acceptance by the country concerned of such recommended increases shall be subject to the unanimous approval of the High Contracting Parties to the present Protocol expressed either in the Council of Western European Union or in the North Atlantic Treaty Organization.

Article 4

In order that it may establish that the limits specified in Articles 1 and 2 are being observed, the Council of Western European Union will regularly receive information acquired as a result of inspections carried out by the Supreme Allied Commander Europe. Such information will be transmitted by a high-ranking officer designated for the purpose by the Supreme Allied Commander Europe.

Article 5

The strength and armaments of the internal defence and police forces on the mainland of Europe of the High Contracting Parties to the present Protocol shall be fixed by agreements within the Organization of Western European Union, having regard to their proper functions and needs and to their existing levels.

Article 6

Her Majesty the Queen of the United Kingdom of Great Britain and Northern Ireland will continue to maintain on the mainland of Europe, including Germany, the effective strength of the United Kingdom forces which are now assigned to the Supreme Allied Commander Europe, that is to say four divisions and the Second Tactical Air Force, or such other forces as the Supreme Allied Commander Europe regards as having equivalent fighting capacity. She undertakes not to withdraw these forces against the wishes of the majority of the High Contracting Parties who should take their decision in the knowledge of the views of the Supreme Allied Commander Europe. This undertaking shall not, however, bind her in the event of an acute overseas emergency. If the maintenance of the United Kingdom forces on the mainland of Europe throws at any time too great a strain on the external finances of the United Kingdom, she will, through Her Government in the United Kingdom of Great Britain and Northern Ireland, invite the North Atlantic Council to review the financial conditions on which the United Kingdom formations are maintained.

In witness whereof, the above-mentioned Plenipotentiaries have signed the present Protocol, being one of the Protocols listed in Article I of the Protocol Modifying and Completing the Treaty, and have affixed thereto their seals.

Done at Paris this 23rd day of October, 1954, in two texts, in the English and French languages, each text being equally authoritative, in a single copy, which shall remain deposited in the archives of the Belgian Government and of which certified copies shall be transmitted by that Government to each of the other Signatories.

Document C4

Conference files, lot 60 D 627, CF 392

Draft Resolution To Implement Section IV of the Final Act of the London Conference [1]

CONFIDENTIAL   PARIS, October 19, 1954.

The North Atlantic Council:

1. *Recognising* the necessity of strengthening the structure of the North Atlantic Treaty Organization and of reinforcing the machinery for the collective defence of Europe, and desirous of specifying the conditions governing joint examination of the defence effort of member countries,

2. *Recalls* that:

(*a*) the resources which member nations intend to devote to their defence effort as well as the level, composition and quality of the forces which the member nations are contributing to the defence of the North Atlantic area are each year subject to collective examination in the NATO Annual Review for the purpose of reaching agreement on force goals, taking into account expected mutual aid;

(*b*) the defence expenditures incurred by the member nations and the extent to which the recommendations emerging from the Annual

---

[1] This draft resolution, which was circulated as document C–M(54)85 along with a covering note by Secretary General Ismay, was approved without change by the North Atlantic Council during its meeting on Oct. 22; for a record of that meeting, see p. 1422.

Review have been carried out are the subject of periodical review during the year.

3. *Agrees* with the terms of the Agreement on Forces of Western European Union; and that with respect to the forces which the members of Western European Union will place under NATO Command on the mainland of Europe and for which maximum figures have been established in that Agreement, if at any time during the NATO Annual Review recommendations are put forward, the effect of which would be to increase the level of forces above the limits established in this Agreement, the acceptance by the country concerned of such recommended increases shall be subject to unanimous approval by the members of Western European Union, expressed either in the Council of Western European Union or in the North Atlantic Treaty Organization.

4. *Decides* that all forces of member nations stationed in the area of the Allied Command Europe shall be placed under the authority of the Supreme Allied Commander Europe or other appropriate NATO Command and under the direction of the NATO military authorities with the exception of those forces intended for the defence of overseas territories and other forces which the North Atlantic Treaty Organization has recognised or will recognise as suitable to remain under national command.

5. *Invites* member nations to make an initial report for consideration and recognition by the Council on those forces which they plan to maintain within the area of Allied Command Europe for the common defence, but not to place under the authority of the North Atlantic Treaty Organization, taking into account the provisions of relevant NATO directives bearing on that subject; the initial report will include a broad statement of the reason for which the above forces are not so placed. Thereafter, if any changes are proposed, the North Atlantic Council action on the NATO Annual Review will constitute recognition as to the suitability and size of forces to be placed under the authority of the appropriate NATO Command and those to be retained under national command.

6. *Notes* that the agreements concluded within the framework of the Organization of Western European Union on the internal defence and police forces which the members of that Organization will maintain on the mainland shall be notified to the North Atlantic Council.

7. *Agrees*, in the interest of most effective collective defence, that in respect of combat forces in the area of Allied Command Europe and under the Supreme Allied Commander Europe;

(*a*) all deployments shall be in accordance with NATO strategy;

117

(*b*) the location of forces in accordance with NATO operational plans shall be determined by the Supreme Allied Commander Europe after consultation and agreement with the national authorities concerned;

(*c*) forces under the Supreme Allied Commander Europe and within the area of Allied Command Europe shall not be redeployed or used operationally within that area without the consent of the Supreme Allied Commander Europe, subject to political guidance furnished by the North Atlantic Council, when appropriate, through normal channels.

8. *Decides* that:

(*a*) integration of forces at Army Group and Tactical Air Force level shall be maintained;

(*b*) in view of the powerful combat support units and logistic support organization at Army level, integration at that level and associated Air Force level will be the rule, wherever formations of several nationalities are operating in the same area and on a common task, provided there are no overriding objections from the point of view of military effectiveness;

(*c*) wherever military efficiency permits, in light of the size, location and logistic support of forces, integration at lower levels, both in the land and air forces, shall be achieved to the maximum extent possible;

(*d*) proposals to the North Atlantic Council, indicating any increases in commonly financed items of expenditure, such as infrastructure which might be entailed by the adoption of such measures, should be submitted by the NATO military authorities.

9. *Agrees* that, in order to improve the capability of the Supreme Allied Commander Europe to discharge his responsibilities in the defence of Allied Command Europe, his responsibilities and powers for the logistic support of the forces placed under his authority shall be extended.

10. *Considers* that these increased responsibilities and powers should include authority:

(*a*) to establish, in consultation with the national authorities concerned, requirements for the provision of logistic resources;*

(*b*) to determine, in agreement with the national authorities concerned, their geographic distribution;

(*c*) to establish, in consultation with these authorities, logistic priorities for the raising, equipping and maintenance of units;

(*d*) to direct the utilisation, for meeting his requirements, of those portions of the logistic support systems made available to him by the appropriate authorities;

(*e*) to co-ordinate and supervise the use, for logistical purposes, of

---

*By logistic resources should be understood all the matériel, supplies, installations and parts thereof necessary for the prolonged conduct of combat operations. [Footnote in the source text.]

NATO common infrastructure facilities and of those national facilities made available to him by the national authorities.

11. *Agrees* that in order to ensure that adequate information is obtained and made available to the appropriate authorities about the forces placed under the Supreme Allied Commander Europe including reserve formations and their logistic support within the area of Allied Command Europe, the Supreme Allied Commander Europe shall be granted increased authority to call for reports regarding the level and effectiveness of such forces and their armaments, equipment and supplies as well as the organization and location of their logistic arrangements. He shall also make field inspections within that area as necessary.

12. *Invites* nations to submit to the Supreme Allied Commander Europe such reports to this end as he may call for from time to time; and to assist inspection within the area of Allied Command Europe by the Supreme Allied Commander Europe of these forces and their logistic support arrangements as necessary.

13. *Confirms* that the powers exercised by the Supreme Allied Commander Europe in peacetime extend not only to the organization into an effective integrated force of the forces placed under him but also to their training; that in this field, the Supreme Allied Commander Europe has direct control over the higher training of all national forces assigned to his command in peacetime; and that he should receive facilities from member nations to inspect the training of those cadre and other forces within the area of Allied Command Europe earmarked for that Command.

14. *Directs* the NATO military authorities to arrange for the designation by the Supreme Allied Commander Europe of a high-ranking officer of his Command who will be authorised to transmit regularly to the Council of Western European Union information relating to the forces of the members of Western European Union on the mainland of Europe acquired as a result of the reports and inspections mentioned in paragraphs 11 and 12 in order to enable that Council to establish that the limits laid down in the special agreement mentioned in paragraph 3 above are being observed.

15. *Agrees* that the expression "the area of Allied Command Europe" as used throughout this resolution shall not include North Africa; and that this Resolution does not alter the present status of the United Kingdom and United States forces in the Mediterranean.

16. *Directs* the NATO Military Committee to initiate the necessary changes in the directives to give effect to the above policies and objectives of the North Atlantic Council.

Document C5

Final Act of the Conference on Security and Co-operation in Europe, Helsinki, August 1, 1975 [1]

The Conference on Security and Co-operation in Europe, which opened at Helsinki on 3 July 1973 and continued at Geneva from 18 September 1973 to 21 July 1975, was concluded at Helsinki on 1 August 1975 by the High Representatives of Austria, Belgium, Bulgaria, Canada, Cyprus, Czechoslovakia, Denmark, Finland, France, the German Democratic Republic, the Federal Republic of Germany, Greece, the Holy See, Hungary, Iceland, Ireland, Italy, Liechtenstein, Luxembourg, Malta, Monaco, the Netherlands, Norway, Poland, Portugal, Romania, San Marino, Spain, Sweden, Switzerland, Turkey, the Union of Soviet Socialist Republics, the United Kingdom, the United States of America and Yugoslavia.

During the opening and closing stages of the Conference the participants were addressed by the Secretary-General of the United Nations as their guest of honour. The Director-General of UNESCO

---

[1] "Conference on Security and Co-operation in Europe, Final Act, Helsinki 1975," Department of State publication 8826, General Foreign Policy Series 298 (August 1975).

and the Executive Secretary of the United Nations Economic Commission for Europe addressed the Conference during its second stage.

During the meetings of the second stage of the Conference contributions were received, and statements heard, from the following non-participating Mediterranean States on various agenda items: the Democratic and Popular Republic of Algeria, the Arab Republic of Egypt, Israel, the Kingdom of Morocco, the Syrian Arab Republic, Tunisia.

Motivated by the political will, in the interest of peoples, to improve and intensify their relations and to contribute in Europe to peace, security, justice and co-operation as well as to rapprochement among themselves and with the other States of the World,

Determined, in consequence, to give full effect to the results of the Conference and to assure, among their States and throughout Europe, the benefits deriving from those results and thus to broaden, deepen and make continuing and lasting the process of détente,

The High Representatives of the participating States have solemnly adopted the following:

QUESTIONS RELATING TO SECURITY IN EUROPE

The States participating in the Conference on Security and Co-operation in Europe,

Reaffirming their objective of promoting better relations among themselves and ensuring conditions in which their people can live in true and lasting peace free from any threat to or attempt against their security;

Convinced of the need to exert efforts to make détente both a continuing and an increasingly viable and comprehensive process, universal in scope, and that the implementation of the results of the Conference on Security and Co-operation in Europe will be a major contribution to this process;

Considering that solidarity among peoples, as well as the common purpose of the participating States in achieving the aims as set forth by the Conference on Security and Co-operation in Europe, should lead to the development of better and closer relations among them in all fields and thus to overcoming the confrontation stemming from the character of their past relations, and to better mutual understanding;

Mindful of their common history and recognizing that the existence of elements common to their traditions and values can assist them in developing their relations, and desiring to search, fully taking into account the individuality and diversity of their positions and views, for possibilities of joining their efforts with a view to overcoming distrust and increasing confidence, solving the problems that separate them and co-operating in the interest of mankind;

Recognizing the indivisibility of security in Europe as well as their common interest in development of co-operation throughout Europe and among themselves and expressing their intention to pursue efforts accordingly;

Recognizing the close link between peace and security in Europe and in the world as a whole and conscious of the need for each of them to make its contribution to the strengthening of world peace and security and to the promotion of fundamental rights, economic and social progress and well-being for all peoples;
Have adopted the following:

1.

(A) DECLARATION ON PRINCIPLES GUIDING RELATIONS BETWEEN PARTICIPATING STATES

The participating States,

Reaffirming their commitment to peace, security and justice and the continuing development of friendly relations and co-operation;
Recognizing that this commitment, which reflects the interest and aspirations of peoples, constitutes for each participating State a present and future responsibility, heightened by experience of the past;
Reaffirming, in conformity with their membership in the United Nations and in accordance with the purposes and principles of the United Nations, their full and active support for the United Nations and for the enhancement of its role and effectiveness in strengthening international peace, security and justice, and in promoting the solution of international problems, as well as the development of friendly relations and co-operation among States;
Expressing their common adherence to the principles which are set forth below and are in conformity with the Charter of the United Nations, as well as their common will to act, in the application of these principles, in conformity with the purposes and principles of the Charter of the United Nations;
Declare their determination to respect and put into practice, each of them in its relations with all other participating States, irrespective of their political, economic or social systems as well as of their size, geographical location or level of economic development, the following principles, which all are of primary significance, guiding their mutual relations:

I. Sovereign equality, respect for the rights inherent in sovereignty

The participating States will respect each other's sovereign equality and individuality as well as all the rights inherent in and encompassed by its sovereignty, including in particular the right of every State to juridical equality, to territorial integrity and to freedom and political independence. They will also respect each other's right freely to choose and develop its political, social, economic and cultural systems as well as its right to determine its laws and regulations.

Within the framework of international law, all the participating States have equal rights and duties. They will respect each other's right to define and conduct as it wishes its relations with other States in accordance with international law and in the spirit of the present Declaration. They consider that their frontiers can be changed, in accordance with international law, by peaceful means

122

and by agreement. They also have the right to belong or not to belong to international organizations, to be or not to be a party to bilateral or multilateral treaties including the right to be or not to be a party to treaties of alliance; they also have the right to neutrality.

II. Refraining from the threat or use of force

The participating States will refrain in their mutual relations, as well as in their international relations in general, from the threat or use of force against the territorial integrity or political independence of any State, or in any other manner inconsistent with the purposes of the United Nations and with the present Declaration. No consideration may be invoked to serve to warrant resort to the threat or use of force in contravention of this principle.

Accordingly, the participating States will refrain from any acts constituting a threat of force or direct or indirect use of force against another participating State. Likewise they will refrain from any manifestation of force for the purpose of inducing another participating State to renounce the full exercise of its sovereign rights. Likewise they will also refrain in their mutual relations from any act of reprisal by force.

No such threat or use of force will be employed as a means of settling disputes, or questions likely to give rise to disputes, between them.

III. Inviolability of frontiers

The participating States regard as inviolable all one another's frontiers as well as the frontiers of all States in Europe and therefore they will refrain now and in the future from assaulting those frontiers.

Accordingly, they will also refrain from any demand for, or act of, seizure and usurpation of part or all of the territory of any participating State.

IV. Territorial integrity of States

The participating States will respect the territorial integrity of each of the participating States.

Accordingly, they will refrain from any action inconsistent with the purposes and principles of the Charter of the United Nations against the territorial integrity, political independence or the unity of any participating State, and in particular from any such action constituting a threat or use of force.

The participating States will likewise refrain from making each other's territory the object of military occupation or other direct or indirect measures of force in contravention of international law, or the object of acquisition by means of such measures or the threat of them. No such occupation or acquisition will be recognized as legal.

V. Peaceful settlement of disputes

The participating States will settle disputes among them by peaceful means in such a manner as not to endanger international peace and security, and justice.

123

They will endeavour in good faith and a spirit of co-operation to reach a rapid and equitable solution on the basis of international law.

For this purpose they will use such means as negotiation, enquiry, mediation, conciliation, arbitration, judicial settlement or other peaceful means of their own choice including any settlement procedure agreed to in advance of disputes to which they are parties.

In the event of failure to reach a solution by any of the above peaceful means, the parties to a dispute will continue to seek a mutually agreed way to settle the dispute peacefully.

Participating States, parties to a dispute among them, as well as other participating States, will refrain from any action which might aggravate the situation to such a degree as to endanger the maintenance of international peace and security and thereby make a peaceful settlement of the dispute more difficult.

VI. Non-intervention in internal affairs

The participating States will refrain from any intervention, direct or indirect, individual or collective, in the internal or external affairs falling within the domestic jurisdiction of another participating State, regardless of their mutual relations.

They will accordingly refrain from any form of armed intervention or threat of such intervention against another participating State.

They will likewise in all circumstances refrain from any other act of military, or of political, economic or other coercion designed to subordinate to their own interest the exercise by another participating State of the rights inherent in its sovereignty and thus to secure advantages of any kind.

Accordingly, they will, inter alia, refrain from direct or indirect assistance to terrorist activities, or to subversive or other activities directed towards the violent overthrow of the regime of another participating State.

VII. Respect for human rights and fundamental freedoms, including the freedom of thought, conscience, religion or belief

The participating States will respect human rights and fundamental freedoms, including the freedom of thought, conscience, religion or belief, for all without distinction as to race, sex, language or religion.

They will promote and encourage the effective exercise of civil, political, economic, social, cultural and other rights and freedoms all of which derive from the inherent dignity of the human person and are essential for his free and full development.

Within this framework the participating States will recognize and respect the freedom of the individual to profess and practise, alone or in community with others, religion or belief acting in accordance with the dictates of his own conscience.

The participating States on whose terrritory national minorities exist will respect the right of persons belonging to such minorities to equality before the law, will afford them the full opportunity for the actual enjoyment of human rights and fundamental freedoms and will, in this manner, protect their legitimate interests in this sphere.

The participating States recognize the universal significance of human rights and fundamental freedoms, respect for which is an essential factor for the peace, justice and well-being necessary to ensure the development of friendly relations and co-operation among themselves as among all States.

They will constantly respect these rights and freedoms in their mutual relations and will endeavour jointly and separately, including in co-operation with the United Nations, to promote universal and effective respect for them.

They confirm the right of the individual to know and act upon his rights and duties in this field.

In the field of human rights and fundamental freedoms, the participating States will act in conformity with the purposes and principles of the Charter of the United Nations and with the Universal Declaration of Human Rights. They will also fulfil their obligations as set forth in the international declarations and agreements in this field, including inter alia the International Covenants on Human Rights by which they may be bound.

VIII. Equal rights and self-determination of peoples

The participating States will respect the equal rights of peoples and their right to self-determination, acting at all times in conformity with the purposes and principles of the Charter of the United Nations and with the relevant norms of international law, including those relating to territorial integrity of States.

By virtue of the principle of equal rights and self-determination of peoples, all peoples always have the right, in full freedom, to determine, when and as they wish, their internal and external political status, without external interference, and to pursue as they wish their political, economic, social and cultural development.

The participating States reaffirm the universal significance of respect for and effective exercise of equal rights and self-determination of peoples for the development of friendly relations among themselves as among all States; they also recall the importance of the elimination of any form of violation of this principle.

IX. Co-operation among States

The participating States will develop their co-operation with one another and with all States in all fields in accordance with the purposes and principles of the Charter of the United Nations. In developing their co-operation the participating States will place special emphasis on the fields as set forth within the framework of the Conference on Security and Co-operation in Europe, with each of them making its contribution in conditions of full equality.

They will endeavour, in developing their co-operation as equals, to promote mutual understanding and confidence, friendly and good-neighbourly relations among themselves, international peace, security and justice. They will equally endeavour, in developing their co-operation, to improve the well-being of peoples and contribute to the fulfilment of their aspirations through, inter alia, the benefits resulting from increased mutual knowledge and from progress and achievement in the economic, scientific, technological, social, cultural and humanitarian fields. They will take steps to promote conditions favourable to making these benefits available to all; they will take into account the interest of all in the narrowing of differences in the levels of economic development, and in particular the interest of developing countries throughout the world.

They confirm that governments, institutions, organizations and persons have a relevant and positive role to play in contributing toward the achievement of these aims of their co-operation.

They will strive, in increasing their co-operation as set forth above, to develop closer relations among themselves on an improved and more enduring basis for the benefit of peoples.

X. Fulfilment in good faith of obligations under international law

The participating States will fulfil in good faith their obligations under international law, both those obligations arising from the generally recognized principles and rules of international law and those obligations arising from treaties or other agreements, in conformity with international law, to which they are parties.

In exercising their sovereign rights, including the right to determine their laws and regulations, they will conform with their legal obligations under international law; they will furthermore pay due regard to and implement the provisions in the Final Act of the Conference on Security and Co-operation in Europe.

The participating States confirm that in the event of a conflict between the obligations of the members of the United Nations under the Charter of the United Nations and their obligations under any treaty or other international agreement, their obligations under the Charter will prevail, in accordance with Article 103 of the Charter of the United Nations.

All the principles set forth above are of primary significance and, accordingly, they will be equally and unreservedly applied, each of them being interpreted taking into account the others.

The participating States express their determination fully to respect and apply these principles, as set forth in the present Declaration, in all aspects, to their mutual relations and co-operation in order to ensure to each participating State the benefits resulting from the respect and application of these principles by all.

The participating States, paying due regard to the principles above and, in particular, to the first sentence of the tenth principle, "Fulfilment in good faith of obligations under international law", note that the present Declaration does not affect their rights and obligations, nor the corresponding treaties and other agreements and arrangements.

The participating States express the conviction that respect for these principles will encourage the development of normal and friendly relations and the progress of co-operation among them in all fields. They also express the conviction that respect for these principles will encourage the development of political contacts among them which in turn would contribute to better mutual understanding of their positions and views.

126

The participating States declare their intention to conduct their relations with all other States in the spirit of the principles contained in the present Declaration.

(B) MATTERS RELATED TO GIVING EFFECT TO CERTAIN OF THE ABOVE PRINCIPLES

(i) The participating States,

Reaffirming that they will respect and give effect to refraining from the threat or use of force and convinced of the necessity to make it an effective norm of international life,

Declare that they are resolved to respect and carry out, in their relations with one another, inter alia, the following provisions which are in conformity with the Declaration on Principles Guiding Relations between Participating States:

—To give effect and expression, by all the ways and forms which they consider appropriate, to the duty to refrain from the threat or use of force in their relations with one another.

—To refrain from any use of armed forces inconsistent with the purposes and principles of the Charter of the United Nations and the provisions of the Declaration on Principles Guiding Relations between the Participating States, against another participating State, in particular from invasion of or attack on its territory.

—To refrain from any manifestation of force for the purpose of inducing another participating State to renounce the full exercise of its sovereign rights.

—To refrain from any act of economic coercion designed to subordinate to their own interest the exercise by another participating State of the rights inherent in its sovereignty and thus to secure advantages of any kind.

—To take effective measures which by their scope and by their nature constitute steps towards the ultimate achievement of general and complete disarmament under strict and effective international control.

—To promote, by all means which each of them considers appropriate, a climate of confidence and respect among peoples consonant with their duty to refrain from propaganda for wars of aggression or for any threat or use of force inconsistent with the purposes of the United Nations and with the Declaration on Principles Guiding Relations between Participating States, against another participating State.

—To make an effort to settle exclusively by peaceful means any dispute between them, the continuance of which is likely to endanger the maintenance of international peace and security in Europe, and to seek, first of all, a solution through the peaceful means set forth in Article 33 of the United Nations Charter.

—To refrain from any action which could hinder the peaceful settlement of disputes between the participating States.

(ii) The participating States,

Reaffirming their determination to settle their disputes as set forth in the Principle of Peaceful Settlement of Disputes;

Convinced that the peaceful settlement of disputes is a complement to refraining from the threat or use of force, both being essential though not exclusive factors for the maintenance and consolidation of peace and security;

Desiring to reinforce and to improve the methods at their disposal for the peaceful settlement of disputes:

1. Are resolved to pursue the examination and elaboration of a generally acceptable method for the peaceful settlement of disputes aimed at complementing existing methods, and to continue to this end to work upon the "Draft Convention on a European System for the Peaceful Settlement of Disputes" submitted by Switzerland during the second stage of the Conference on Security and Co-operation in Europe, as well as other proposals relating to it and directed towards the elaboration of such a method.

2. Decide that, on the invitation of Switzerland, a meeting of experts of all the participating States will be convoked in order to fulfil the mandate described in paragraph 1 above within the framework and under the procedures of the followup to the Conference laid down in the chapter "Follow-up to the Conference".

3. This meeting of experts will take place after the meeting of the representatives appointed by the Ministers of Foreign Affairs of the participating States, scheduled according to the chapter "Follow-up to the Conference" for 1977; the results of the work of this meeting of experts will be submitted to Governments.

2.

DOCUMENT ON CONFIDENCE-BUILDING MEASURES AND CERTAIN ASPECTS OF SECURITY AND DISARMAMENT

The participating States,

Desirous of eliminating the causes of tension that may exist among them and thus of contributing to the strengthening of peace and security in the world;

Determined to strengthen confidence among them and thus to contribute to increasing stability and security in Europe;

Determined further to refrain in their mutual relations, as well as in their international relations in general, from the threat or use of force against the territorial integrity or political independence of any State, or in any other manner inconsistent with the purposes of the United Nations and with the Declaration on Principles Guiding Relations between Participating States as adopted in this Final Act;

Recognizing the need to contribute to reducing the dangers of armed conflict and of misunderstanding or miscalculation of military activities which could give rise to apprehension, particularly in a situation where the participating States lack clear and timely information about the nature of such activities;

Taking into account considerations relevant to efforts aimed at lessening tension and promoting disarmament;

Recognizing that the exchange of observers by invitation at military manoeuvres will help to promote contacts and mutual understanding;

Having studied the question of prior notification of major military movements in the context of confidence-building;

Recognizing that there are other ways in which individual States can contribute further to their common objectives;

Convinced of the political importance of prior notification of major military manoeuvres for the promotion of mutual understanding and the strengthening of confidence, stability and security;

Accepting the responsibility of each of them to promote these objectives and to implement this measure, in accordance with the accepted criteria and modalities, as essentials for the realization of these objectives;

Recognizing that this measure deriving from political decision rests upon a voluntary basis;

Have adopted the following:

I

Prior notification of major military manoeuvres

They will notify their major military manoeuvres to all other participating States through usual diplomatic channels in accordance with the following provisions:

Notification will be given of major military manoeuvres exceeding a total of 25,000 troops, independently or combined with any possible air or naval components (in this context the word "troops" includes amphibious and airborne troops). In the case of independent manoeuvres of amphibious or airborne troops, or of combined manoeuvres involving them, these troops will be included in this total. Furthermore, in the case of combined manoeuvres which do not reach the above total but which involve land forces together with significant numbers of either amphibious or airborne troops, or both, notification can also be given.

Notification will be given of major military manoeuvres which take place on the territory, in Europe, of any participating State as well as, if applicable, in the adjoining sea area and air space.

In the case of a participating State whose territory extends beyond Europe, prior notification need be given only of manoeuvres which take place in an area within 250 kilometres from its frontier facing or shared with any other European participating State. The participating State need not, however, give notification in cases in which that area is also contiguous to the participating State's frontier facing or shared with a non-European non-participating State.

Notification will be given 21 days or more in advance of the start of the manoeuvre or in the case of a manoeuvre arranged at shorter notice at the earliest possible opportunity prior to its starting date.

Notification will contain information of the designation, if any, the general purpose of and the States involved in the manoeuvre, the type or types and numerical strength of the forces engaged, the area and estimated time-frame of its conduct. The participating States will also, if possible, provide additional relevant information, particularly that related to the components of the forces engaged and the period of involvement of these forces.

Prior notification of other military manoeuvres

The participating States recognize that they can contribute further to strengthening confidence and increasing security and stability, and to this end may also notify smaller-scale military manoeuvres to other participating States, with special regard for those near the area of such manoeuvres.

To the same end, the participating States also recognize that they may notify other military manoeuvres conducted by them.

Exchange of observers

The participating States will invite other participating States, voluntarily and on a bilateral basis, in a spirit of reciprocity and goodwill towards all participating States, to send observers to attend military manoeuvres.

The inviting State will determine in each case the number of observers, the procedures and conditions of their participation, and give other information which it may consider useful. It will provide appropriate facilities and hospitality

The invitation will be given as far ahead as is conveniently possible through usual diplomatic channels.

Prior notification of major military movements

In accordance with the Final Recommendations of the Helsinki Consultations the participating States studied the question of prior notification of major military movements as a measure to strengthen confidence.

Accordingly, the participating States recognize that they may, at their own discretion and with a view to contributing to confidence-building, notify their major military movements.

In the same spirit, further consideration will be given by the States participating in the Conference on Security and Co-operation in Europe to the question of prior notification of major military movements, bearing in mind, in particular, the experience gained by the implementation of the measures which are set forth in this document.

Other confidence-building measures

The participating States recognize that there are other means by which their common objectives can be promoted.

In particular, they will, with due regard to reciprocity and with a view to better mutual understanding, promote exchanges by invitation among their military personnel, including visits by military delegations.

In order to make a fuller contribution to their common objective of confidence-building, the participating States, when conducting their military activities in the area covered by the provisions for the prior notification of major military manoeuvres, will duly take into account and respect this objective.

They also recognize that the experience gained by the implementation of the provisions set forth above, together with further efforts, could lead to developing and enlarging measures aimed at strengthening confidence.

II

Questions relating to disarmament

The participating States recognize the interest of all of them in efforts aimed at lessening military confrontation and promoting disarmament which are designed to complement political détente in Europe and to strengthen their security. They are convinced of the necessity to take effective measures in these fields which by their scope and by their nature constitute steps towards the ultimate achievement of general and complete disarmament under strict and effective international control, and which should result in strengthening peace and security throughout the world.

III

General considerations

Having considered the views expressed on various subjects related to the strengthening of security in Europe through joint efforts aimed at promoting détente and disarmament, the participating States, when engaged in such efforts, will, in this context, proceed, in particular, from the following essential considerations:

—The complementary nature of the political and military aspects of security;

—The interrelation between the security of each participating State and security in Europe as a whole and the relationship which exists, in the broader context of world security, between security in Europe and security in the Mediterranean area;

—Respect for the security interests of all States participating in the Conference on Security and Co-operation in Europe inherent in their sovereign equality;

The importance that participants in negotiating fora see to it that information about relevant developments, progress and results is provided on an appropriate basis to other States participating in the Conference on Security and Co-operation in Europe and, in return, the justified interest of any of those States in having their views considered.

Appendix D. Bilateral Agreements

D1. Agreement Between the Military Liaison Missions Accredited to the Soviet and United States Commanders-in-Chief of the Zones of Occupation in Germany, April 5, 1947

D2. Statement by the Soviet Union Attributing Full Sovereignty to the German Democratic Republic, March 25, 1954

D3. Treaty on Relations Between the Soviet Union and the German Democratic Republic, Signed at Moscow, September 20, 1955

D4. Soviet–East German Treaty on Friendship, Mutual Assistance, and Cooperation, Signed at Moscow, June 12, 1964

Document D1

Agreement Between the Military Liaison Missions Accredited to the Soviet and United States Commanders-in-Chief of the Zones of Occupation in Germany, April 5, 1947 [1]

In conformity with the provisions of Article 2 of the Agreement on "Control Mechanism in Germany," November 14, 1944,[2] the US and the Soviet Commanders-in-Chief of the Zones of Occupation in Germany have agreed to exchange Military Liaison Missions accredited to their staffs in the zones and approve the following regulations concerning these missions:

---

[1] Department of State files.
[2] *Ante.*

1. These missions are military missions and have no authority over quadri-partite military government missions or purely military government missions of each respective country, either temporarily or permanently, on duty in either zone. However, they will render whatever aid or assistance to said military government missions as is practicable.

2. Missions will be composed of air, navy, and army representatives. There will be no political representatives.

3. The missions will consist of not to exceed fourteen (14) officers and enlisted personnel. This number will include all necessary technical personnel, office clerks, personnel with special qualifications, and personnel required to operate radio stations.

4. Each mission will be under the orders of senior member of the mission who will be appointed and known as "Chief of the United States (or Soviet) Military Mission."

5. The Chief of the Mission will be accredited to the Commander-in-Chief of the occupation forces.

In the United States Zone the mission will be accredited to Commander-in-Chief, United States European Command.

In the Soviet Zone the mission will be accredited to the Commander-in-Chief of the Group of Soviet Occupational Forces in Germany.

6. In the United States Zone the Soviet Mission will be offered quarters in the region of Frankfurt.

7. In the Soviet Zone the United States Mission will be offered quarters at or near Potsdam.

8. In the United States Zone the Chief of the Soviet Mission will communicate with A/C of Staff, G–3, United States European Command.

9. In the Soviet Zone the Chief of the United States Mission will communicate with the Senior Officer of the Staff of Commander-in-Chief.

10. Each member of the missions will be given identical travel facilities to include identical permanent passes in Russian and English languages permitting complete freedom of travel wherever and whenever it will be desired over territory and roads in both zones, except places of disposition of military units, without escort or supervision.

Each time any member of the Soviet or United States mission wants to visit United States or Soviet headquarters, military government offices, forces, units, military schools, factories, and enterprises which are under United States or Soviet control, a corresponding request must be made to Director, Operations, Plans, Organization and Training, European Command, or Senior Officer, Headquarters, Group of Soviet Occupational Forces in Germany. Such requests must be acted upon within 24–72 hours.

Members of the missions are permitted allied guests at the headquarters of the respective missions.

11. a. Each mission will have its own radio station for communication with its own headquarters.

b. In each case couriers and messengers will be given facilities for free travel between the headquarters of the mission and headquarters of their respective Commander-in-Chief. These couriers will enjoy the same immunity which is extended to diplomatic couriers.

c. Each mission will be given facilities for telephone communication through the local telephone exchange at the headquarters, and they also will be given facilities such as mail, telephone, telegraph through the existing means of communication when the members of the mission will be traveling within the zone. In case of a breakdown in the radio installation, the zone commanders will render all possible aid and will permit temporary use of their own systems of communication.

12. The necessary rations, P.O.L. supplies and household services for the military missions will be provided for by the headquarters to which accredited, by method of mutual compensation in kind, supplemented by such items as desired to be furnished by their own headquarters.

In addition the respective missions or individual members of the missions may purchase items of Soviet or United States origin which must be paid for in currency specified by the headquarters controlling zone where purchase is made.

13. The buildings of each mission will enjoy full right of extraterritoriality.

14. a. The task of the mission will be to maintain liaison between both Commanders-in-Chief and their staffs.

b. In each zone the mission will have the right to engage in matters of protecting the interests of their nationals and to make representations accordingly as well as in matters of protecting their property interests in the zone where they are located. They have the right to render aid to people of their own country who are visiting the zone where they are accredited.

15. This agreement may be changed or amplified by mutual consent to cover new subjects when the need arises.

16. This agreement is written in Russian and English languages and both texts are authentic.

17. This agreement becomes valid when signed by Deputy Commanders of United States and Soviet Zones of Occupation.

C. R. HUEBNER
Lieutenant-General Huebner
Deputy Commander-in-Chief, European Command

Colonel-General Malinin
Deputy Commander-in-Chief
Chief of Staff of the Group of Soviet Occupation Forces in Germany

Document D2

Statement by the Soviet Union Attributing Full Sovereignty to the German Democratic Republic, March 25, 1954 [1]

The Government of the Soviet Union is unswervingly guided by a desire to contribute to a solution of the German problem in accordance with the interests of strengthening peace and securing the national reunification of Germany on a democratic basis.

These aims must be served by practical measures for a *rapprochement* of Eastern and Western Germany, the holding of free all-German elections, and the conclusion of a peace treaty with Germany.

Despite the efforts of the Soviet Union, no steps towards restoring the national unity of Germany and the conclusion of a peace treaty were taken at the recent Berlin Conference of the Foreign Ministers of the four Powers.

In view of this situation and as a result of negotiations which the Soviet Government has held with the Government of the German Democratic Republic, the Government of the USSR considers it necessary to take at once, even before the unification of Germany and the conclusion of a peace treaty, further steps to meet the interests of the German people, namely:

1. The Soviet Union establishes the same relations with the German Democratic Republic as with other sovereign States.

The German Democratic Republic shall be free to decide on internal and external affairs, including the question of relations with Western Germany, at its discretion.

2. The Soviet Union will retain in the German Democratic Republic the functions connected with guaranteeing security, and resulting from the obligations incumbent on the USSR as a result of the Four-power Agreement. [2]

The Soviet Government has taken note of the statement of the Government of the German Democratic Republic that it will carry out its obligations arising from the Potsdam Agreement on the development of Germany as a democratic and peace-loving State, as well as the obligations connected with the temporary stationing of Soviet troops on the territory of the German Democratic Republic.

3. Supervision of the activities of the German Democratic Republic, hitherto carried out by the High Commissioner of the USSR in Germany, will be abolished.

In accordance with this, the functions of the High Commissioner of the USSR in Germany will be limited to questions mentioned above connected with guaranteeing security and maintaining the appropriate liaison with the representatives of the Occupying Authorities of the USA, Great Britain, and France regarding questions of an all-German character and arising from the agreed decisions of the four Powers on Germany.

The Government of the USSR is of the opinion that the existence of the Occupation Statute laid down for Western Germany by the

United States of America, Great Britain, and France,[3] is not only incompatible with the principles of democracy and the national rights of the German people, but constitutes one of the main obstacles on the road to the national reunification of Germany, by impeding the *rapprochement* between Eastern and Western Germany.

---

[3] See *ante* under dates of April 8 and September 21, 1949, and March 7, 1951.

Document D3

Treaty on Relations Between the Soviet Union and the German Democratic Republic, Signed at Moscow, September 20, 1955 [1]

[Translation]

The Presidium of the Supreme Soviet of the Union of Soviet Socialist Republics and the President of the German Democratic Republic,

Desirous of promoting close co-operation and further strengthening the friendly relations between the Union of Soviet Socialist Republics and the German Democratic Republic on a basis of equality, respect for each other's sovereignty and non-intervention in each other's domestic affairs.

Mindful of the new situation created by the entry into force of the Paris Agreements of 1954.

Convinced that by combining their efforts towards the maintenance and strengthening of international peace and European security, the reunification of Germany as a peaceful and democratic State, and a settlement by peace treaty with Germany, the Soviet Union and the German Democratic Republic will be serving the interests both of the Soviet and German peoples and of the other peoples of Europe.

Having regard to the obligations of the Soviet Union and of the German Democratic Republic under existing international agreements relating to Germany as a whole,

Have decided to conclude the present Treaty and have appointed as their plenipotentiaries:

The Presidium of the Supreme Soviet of the Union of Soviet Socialist Republics: Mr. N. A. Bulganin, Chairman of the Council of Ministers of the USSR;

The President of the German Democratic Republic: Mr. Otto Grotewohl, Prime Minister of the German Democratic Republic;

Who, having exchanged their full powers, found in good and due form, have agreed as follows:

Article 1

The Contracting Parties solemnly reaffirm that the relations between them are based on full equality, respect for each other's sovereignty and non-intervention in each other's domestic affairs.

The German Democratic Republic is accordingly free to take decisions on all questions pertaining to its domestic and foreign policy, including its relations with the Federal Republic of Germany and the development of relations with other States.

Article 2

The Contracting Parties declare their readiness to participate, in a spirit of sincere co-operation, in all international actions designed to ensure peace and security in Europe and throughout the world in conformity with the principles of the United Nations Charter.

---

[1] 226 United Nations Treaty Series 208-212. A footnote in the source text indicates that the Treaty entered into force on October 6, 1955, upon the exchange of the instruments of ratification at Berlin, in accordance with article 7.

To this end they shall consult with each other on all major international questions affecting the interests of the two States and shall adopt all measures within their power to prevent any breach of the peace.

Article 3

In accordance with the interests of the two countries and guided by the principles of friendship, the Contracting Parties agree to develop and strengthen the existing ties between the Union of Soviet Socialist Republics and the German Democratic Republic in economic, scientific, technical and cultural matters, to extend to each other all possible economic assistance, and to co-operate, wherever necessary, in the economic, scientific and technical fields.

Article 4

The Soviet forces now stationed in the territory of the German Democratic Republic in accordance with existing international agreements shall temporarily remain in the German Democratic Republic, with the consent of its Government and subject to conditions which shall be defined in a supplementary agreement between the Government of the Soviet Union and the Government of the German Democratic Republic.

The Soviet forces temporarily stationed in the territory of the German Democratic Republic shall not intervene in the domestic affairs or the social and political life of the German Democratic Republic.

Article 5

The Contracting Parties agree that their fundamental aim is to achieve, through appropriate negotiation, a peaceful settlement for the whole of Germany. They will accordingly make the necessary efforts to achieve a settlement by peace treaty and the reunification of Germany on a peaceful and democratic basis.

Article 6

This Treaty shall remain in force until Germany is re-united as a peaceful and democratic state, or until the Contracting Parties agree that the Treaty should be amended or terminated.

Article 7

This Treaty shall be ratified and shall enter into force on the date of the exchange of the instruments of ratification, which shall take place at Berlin as soon as possible.

Done in duplicate, at Moscow, on 20 September 1955, in the Russian and German languages, both texts being equally authentic.

By authorization of the Presidium of the
Supreme Soviet of the USSR:
N. Bulganin

By authorization of the President of the
German Democratic Republic:
O. Grotewohl

Document D4

Soviet-East German Treaty on Friendship, Mutual Assistance, and Cooperation, Signed at Moscow, June 12, 1964 [1]

The Union of Soviet Socialist Republics and the German Democratic Republic;

Guided by the desire to continue to develop and strengthen the fraternal friendship between the Union of Soviet Socialist Republics and the German Democratic Republic, which is in line with the basic interests of the peoples of both countries and of the commonwealth as a whole;

On the basis of the fraternal all-round cooperation which is the cornerstone of the policy determining the relations between both states and which has assumed a still closer and cordial nature after the conclusion of the treaty on the relations between the Union of Soviet Socialist Republics and the German Democratic Republic of Sept. 20, 1955; [2]

Expressing firm intention to contribute to the cause of consolidating peace in Europe and throughout the world and to follow unswervingly a policy of peaceful coexistence of states with different social systems;

Fully determined to unite their efforts in order to counteract effectively on the basis of the Warsaw Treaty of Friendship, Cooperation and Mutual Assistance of May 14, 1955,[3] the threat to international security and peace created by the revanchist and militarist forces which are striving for a revision of the results of World War II;

And to defend the territorial integrity and sovereignty of both states from any attack;

Being of unanimous opinion that the German Democratic Republic, the first state of workers and peasants in the history of Germany, which has carried into life the principles of the Potsdam agreement and follows the path of peace, is an important factor for insuring security in Europe and aversion of the war threat;

Striving to facilitate the conclusion of a German peace treaty and to conduce to the realization of Germany's unity on peaceful and democratic principles;

[1] *The New York Times,* June 13, 1964 (text as printed in *American Foreign Policy: Current Documents, 1964*, pp. 533–535); this treaty entered into force on September 26, 1964.
[2] *Ante.*
[3] *Ante.*

Guided by the aims and principles of the United Nations Charter;

Agreed on the following:

ARTICLE I

The high contracting parties, on the basis of full equality, mutual respect for the state sovereignty, noninterference in internal affairs and the lofty principles of Socialist internationalism, implementing the principles of mutual advantage and mutual fraternal assistance, will continue to develop and consolidate the relations of friendship and close cooperation in all spheres.

ARTICLE II

In the interests of peace and peaceful future of the peoples, including the German people, the high contracting parties will unswervingly work for the elimination of the remnants of World War II, for the conclusion of a German peace treaty and for the normalization of the situation in West Berlin on this basis.

The sides proceed from the premise that, pending the conclusion of a German peace treaty the United States of America, Great Britain and France continue to bear their responsibility for the realization on the territory of the Federal Republic of Germany of the demands and commitments jointly assumed by the Governments of the four powers under the Potsdam and other international agreements and directed toward the eradication of German militarism and Nazism and toward the prevention of German aggression.

ARTICLE III

The high contracting parties join their efforts directed toward insuring peace and security in Europe and throughout the world in accordance with the aims and principles of the United Nations Charter. They will take all measures in their power to conduce to the settlement on the basis of the principles of peaceful coexistence, of the cardinal international problems such as general and complete disarmament, including partial measures conducing to the discontinuation of the arms-race and relaxation of international tensions, abolition of colonialism, settlement of territorial and border disputes between states by peaceful means, and others.

ARTICLE IV

In the face of the existing danger of an aggressive war on the part of the militarist and revanchist forces the high contracting parties solemnly declare that the integrity of the state frontiers of the German Democratic Republic is one of the basic factors for European security. They confirm their firm determination to guarantee the inviolability of these frontiers in accordance with the Warsaw Treaty on Friendship, Cooperation and Mutual Assistance.

The high contracting parties will also undertake all necessary measures for preventing aggression on the part of the forces of militarism and revanchism which are striving for a revision of the results of World War II.

ARTICLE V

In the case if one of the high contracting parties becomes an object of an armed attack in Europe by some state or a group of states, the other high contracting party will render it immediate assistance in accordance with the provisions of the Warsaw Treaty on Friendship, Cooperation and Mutual Assistance.

The Security Council will be informed of the measures taken, in accordance with the provisions of the United Nations Charter. These measures will be discontinued as soon as the Security Council takes measures necessary for restoring and maintaining international peace and security.

ARTICLE VI

The high contracting parties will regard West Berlin as an independent political unit.

ARTICLE VII

The high contracting parties confirm their opinion that in view of the existence of two sovereign German states—the German Democratic Republic and the Federal Republic of Germany—the creation of a peace-loving democratic united German state can be achieved only through negotiations on an equal footing and agreement between both sovereign German states.

ARTICLE VIII

On the basis of mutual advantage and unselfish fraternal cooperation, in accordance with the principles of the Council of Mutual Economic Assistance [4] the high contracting parties will develop and consolidate in every way the economic, scientific and technical relations between both states, to carry out, in accordance with the principles of international Socialist division of labor, the coordination of national economic plans, specialization and cooperation of production and to insure the highest productivity through a rapprochement and coordination of the national economies of both states.

The sides will continue to develop their relations in the cultural, public and sports fields, and also in the sphere of tourism.

ARTICLE IX

The present treaty does not affect the rights and commitments of the sides under the bilateral and other international agreements which are in force, including the Potsdam agreement.

---

[4] Reference to a secret protocol signed by Bulgaria, Czechoslovakia, Hungary, Poland, Romania, and the U.S.S.R., in Moscow, January 24, 1949; Albania joined the Council on February 22, 1949, the German Democratic Republic, on September 29, 1950; for the text of the communiqué on the establishment of the Council, published January 25, 1949, see *The New York Times*, January 26, 1949. [Footnote in the source text.]

ARTICLE X

This treaty will be valid for 20 years since the day on which it enters into force. The treaty will remain in force for 10 more years if neither of the high contracting parties denunciates it 12 months before the expiration of the treaty's term.

In case of the establishment of a united democratic and peace-loving German state or the conclusion of a German peace treaty, the present treaty can be revised at the request of either of the high contracting parties before the expiration of its 20-year term.

ARTICLE XI

The present treaty is subject to ratification and will enter into force at the moment of the exchange of the ratification instruments, which will take place in Berlin in the nearest future.

Done in Moscow on June 12th, 1964, in two copies, each in the Russian and German languages, both texts being equally valid.

Appendix E. Excerpts from the Basic Law of the FRG

Article 24 (Entry into a collective security system)

(1) The Federation may by legislation transfer sovereign powers to inter-governmental institutions.

(2) For the maintenance of peace, the Federation may enter a system of mutual collective security; in doing so it will consent to such limitations upon its rights of sovereignty as will bring about and secure a peaceful and lasting order in Europe and among the nations of the world.

(3) For the settlement of disputes between states, the Federation will accede to agreements concerning international arbitration of a general, comprehensive and obligatory nature.

Article 26 (Ban on war of aggression)

(1) Acts tending to and undertaken with the intent to disturb the peaceful relations between nations, especially to prepare for aggressive war, shall be unconstitutional. They shall be made a punishable offence.

(2) Weapons designed for warfare may not be manufactured, transported or marketed except with the permission of the Federal Government. Details shall be regulated by a federal law.

Article 87a ** (Build-up, strength, use and functions of the Armed Forces)

(1) The Federation shall build up Armed Forces for defence purposes. Their numerical strength and general organizational structure shall be shown in the budget.

(2) Apart from defence, the Armed Forces may only be used to the extent explicitly permitted by this Basic Law.

(3) While a state of defence or a state of tension exists, the Armed Forces shall have the power to protect civilian property and discharge functions of traffic control in so far as this is necessary for the performance of their defence mission. Moreover, the Armed Forces may, when a state of defence or a state of tension exists, be entrusted with the protection of civilian property in support of police measures; in this event the Armed Forces shall co-operate with the competent authorities.

(4) In order to avert any imminent danger to the existence or to the free democratic basic order of the Federation or a Land, the Federal Government may, should conditions as envisaged in paragraph (2) of Article 91 obtain and the police forces and the Federal Border Guard be inadequate, use the Armed Forces to support the police and the Federal Border Guard in the protection of civilian property and in combatting organized and militarily armed insurgents. Any such use of Armed Forces must be discontinued whenever the Bundestag or the Bundesrat so requests.

Article 115 a (Determination of a state of defence)

(1) The determination that the federal territory is being attacked by armed force or that such an attack is directly imminent (state of defence) shall be made by the Bundestag with the consent of the Bundesrat. Such determination shall be made at the request of the Federal Government and shall require a two-thirds majority of the votes cast, which shall include at least the majority of the members of the Bundestag.

(2) If the situation imperatively calls for immediate action and if insurmountable obstacles prevent the timely meeting of the Bundestag, or if there is no quorum in the Bundestag, the Joint Committee shall make this determination with a two-thirds majority of the votes cast, which shall include at least the majority of its members.

(3) The determination shall be promulgated in the Federal Law Gazette by the Federal President pursuant to Article 82. If this cannot be done in time, the promulgation shall be effected in another manner; it shall subsequently be printed in the Federal Law Gazette as soon as circumstances permit.

(4) If the Federal territory is being attacked by armed force and if the competent organs of the Federation are not in a position at once to make the determination provided for in the first sentence of paragraph (1) of this Article, such determination shall be deemed to have been made and promulgated at the time the attack began. The Federal President shall announce such time as soon as circumstances permit.

(5) When the determination of the existence of a state of defence has been promulgated and if the federal territory is being attacked by armed force, the Federal President may, with the consent of the Bundestag, issue internationally valid declarations regarding the existence of such state of defence. Subject to the conditions mentioned in paragraph (2) of this Article, the Joint Committee shall thereupon deputize for the Bundestag.

Article 115b (Power of command during state of defence)

Upon the promulgation of a state of defence, the power of command over the Armed Forces shall pass to the Federal Chancellor.

Article 115c (Legislative competence of the Federation during state of defence)

(1) The Federation shall have the right to exercise concurrent legislation even in matters belonging to the legislative competence of the Laender by enacting laws to be applicable upon the occurrence of a state of defence. Such laws shall require the consent of the Bundesrat.

(2) Federal legislation to be applicable upon the occurrence of a state of defence to the extent required by conditions obtaining while such state of defence exists, may make provision for:

1. preliminary compensation to be made in the event of expropriations, thus diverging from the second sentence of paragraph (3) of Article 14;

2. deprivations of liberty for a period not exceeding four days, if no judge has been able to act within the period applying in normal times, thus diverging from the third sentence of paragraph (2) and the first sentence of paragraph (3) of Article 104.

(3)* Federal legislation to be applicable upon the occurrence of a state of defence to the extent required for averting an existing or directly imminent attack, may, subject to the consent of the Bundesrat, regulate the administration and the fiscal system of the Federation and the Laender in divergence from Sections VIII, VIIIa and X, provided that the viability of the Laender, communes and associations of communes is safeguarded, particularly in fiscal matters.

(4) Federal laws enacted pursuant to paragraph (1) or subparagraph (1) of paragraph (2) of this Article may, for the purpose of preparing for their execution, be applied even prior to the occurrence of a state of defence.

Article 115d (Shortened procedure in the case of urgent bills during state of defence)

(1) While a state of defence exists, the provisions of paragraphs (2) and (3) of this Article shall apply in respect of federal legislation, notwithstanding the provisions of paragraph (2) of Article 76, the second sentence of paragraph (1) and paragraphs (2) to (4) of Article 77, Article 78, and paragraph (1) of Article 82.

(2) Bills submitted as urgent by the Federal Government shall be forwarded to the Bundesrat at the same time as they are submitted to the Bundestag. The Bundestag and the Bundesrat shall debate such bills in common without delay. In so far as the consent of the Bundesrat is necessary, the majority of its votes shall be required for any such bill to become a law. Details shall be regulated by rules of procedure adopted by the Bundestag and requiring the consent of the Bundesrat.

(3) The second sentence of paragraph (3) of Article 115a shall apply mutatis mutandis in respect of the promulgation of such laws.

Article 115e (Status and functions of the Joint Committee)

(1) If, while a state of defence exists, the Joint Committee determines with a two-thirds majority of the votes cast, which shall include at least the majority of its members, that insurmountable obstacles prevent the timely meeting of the Bundestag, or that there is no quorum in the Bundestag, the Joint Committee shall have the status of both the Bundestag and the Bundesrat and shall exercise their rights as one body.

(2) The Joint Committee may not enact any law to amend this Basic Law or to deprive it of effect or application either in whole or in part. The Joint Committee shall not be authorized to enact laws pursuant to paragraph (1) of Article 24 or to Article 29.

Article 115f (Extraordinary powers of the Federation during state of defence)

(1) While a state of defence exists, the Federal Government may to the extent necessitated by circumstances:

1. commit the Federal Border Guard throughout the federal territory;
2. issue instructions not only to federal administrative authorities but also to Land governments and, if it deems the matter urgent, to Land authorities, and may delegate this power to members of Land governments to be designated by it.

(2) The Bundestag, the Bundesrat, and the Joint Committee, shall be informed without delay of the measures taken in accordance with paragraph (1) of this Article.

Article 115g (Status and functions of the Federal Constitutional Court during state of defence)

The constitutional status and the exercise of the constitutional functions of the Federal Constitutional Court and its judges must not be impaired. The Law on the Federal Constitutional Court may not be amended by a law enacted by the Joint Committee except in so far as such amendment is required, also in the opinion of the Federal Constitutional Court, to maintain the capability of the Court to function. Pending the enactment of such a law, the Federal Constitutional Court may take such measures as are necessary to maintain the capability of the Court to carry out its work. Any decisions by the Federal Constitutional Court in pursuance of the second and third sentences of this Article shall require a two-thirds majority of the judges present.

Article 115h (Legislative terms and terms of office during state of defence)

(1) Any legislative terms of the Bundestag or of Land diets due to expire while a state of defence exists shall end six months after the termination of such state of defence. A term of office of the Federal President due to expire while a state of defence exists, and the exercise of his functions by the President of the Bundesrat in case of the premature vacancy of the Federal President's office, shall end nine months after the termination of such state of defence. The term of office of a member of the Federal Constitutional Court due to expire while a state of defence exists shall end six months after the termination of such state of defence.

(2) Should the necessity arise for the Joint Committee to elect a new Federal Chancellor, the Committee shall do so with the majority of its members; the Federal President shall propose a candidate to the Joint Committee. The Joint Committee can express its lack of confidence in the Federal Chancellor only by electing a successor with a two-thirds majority of its members.

(3) The Bundestag shall not be dissolved while a state of defence exists.

Article 115i (Extraordinary power of the Land governments)

(1) If the competent federal organs are incapable of taking the measures necessary to avert the danger, and if the situation imperatively calls for immediate independent action in individual parts of the federal territory, the Land governments or the authorities or commissioners designated by them shall be authorized to take, within their respective spheres of competence, the measures provided for in paragraph (1) of Article 115f.

(2) Any measures taken in accordance with paragraph (1) of the present Article may be revoked at any time by the Federal Government, or in the case of Land authorities and subordinate federal authorities, by Land Prime Ministers.

Article 115k (Grade and duration of validity of extraordinary laws and ordinances having the force of law)

(1) Laws enacted in accordance with Articles 115c, 115e, and 115g, as well as ordinances having the force of law issued by virtue of such laws, shall, for the duration of their applicability, suspend legislation contrary to such laws or ordinances. This shall not apply to earlier legislation enacted by virtue of Articles 115c, 115e, or 115g.

(2) Laws adopted by the Joint Committee, and ordinances having the force of law issued by virtue of such laws, shall cease to have effect not later than six months after the termination of a state of defence.

(3)* Laws containing provisions that diverge from Articles 91a, 91b, 104a, 106 and 107, shall apply no longer than the end of the second fiscal year following upon the termination of the state of defence. After such termination they may, with the consent of the Bundesrat, be amended by federal legislation so as to lead up to the settlement provided for in Sections VIII a and X.

Article 115l (Repealing of extraordinary laws, Termination of state of defence, Conclusion of peace)

(1) The Bundestag, with the consent of the Bundesrat, may at any time repeal laws enacted by the Joint Committee. The Bundesrat may request the Bundestag to make a decision in any such matter. Any measures taken by the Joint Committee or the Federal Government to avert a danger shall be revoked if the Bundestag and the Bundesrat so decide.

(2) The Bundestag, with the consent of the Bundesrat, may at any time declare the state of defence terminated by a decision to be promulgated by the Federal President. The Bundesrat may request the Bundestag to make a decision in any such matter. The state of defence must be declared terminated without delay when the prerequisites for the determination thereof no longer exist.

(3) The conclusion of peace shall be the subject of a federal law.

ADDENDUM

On September 12, 1990, the Two plus Four talks were finally concluded in Moscow with the foreign ministers of the six nations signing the Treaty on the Final Settlement with Respect to Germany. Though in deference to German wishes the agreement does not constitute a formal peace treaty, it in effect draws "a line under World War II," to borrow Soviet Foreign Minister Eduard Shevardnadze's phrase. Since the treaty will not be ratified by the time German unification commences on October 3, 1990, the four powers have agreed to suspend their quadripartite rights on October 1. A digest of the principal terms of the treaty follows:

Article 1. The territory of the united Germany will be bounded by the borders of the Federal Republic and the German Democratic Republic. These borders will be "definitive" from the time the treaty enters into force. A separate treaty will be reached between Germany and Poland that confirms the existing border between the two states as binding under international law. The united Germany, moreover, eschews any territorial claims against other states and any future assertions of that nature.

Article 2. This reaffirms earlier declarations that "only peace will emanate from German soil" and underlines the existing constitutional prohibition against aggressive activities undertaken with the intent to disturb peaceful relations with other states. Likewise, the united Germany pledges that it will not use its weapons except in accordance with the constitution and the U.N. Charter.

Article 3. This also reaffirms previous commitments not to manufacture, possess, or control nuclear, biological, and chemical weapons, which the united Germany will also observe. Similarly, it will abide by the Nuclear Non-Proliferation Treaty. As promised, the united Germany will reduce the strength of its armed forces to a level no higher than 370,000 personnel within three to four years from the time the first CFE agreement enters into force.

Article 4. A separate treaty will be concluded with the Soviet Union that governs the terms and conditions for the departure of Soviet forces from the GDR by the end of 1994.

Article 5. Until Soviet forces complete their withdrawal from the GDR and Berlin, only German territorial defense units not assigned to NATO will be stationed in this territory. The armed forces of other states also cannot be stationed there or be allowed to carry out other military activity there.

The forces of the four powers, however, will be allowed, upon German request, to remain in Berlin during this period but at levels no higher than currently exist. Separate agreements will be reached among the relevant governments to codify the conditions for their continuing presence in Berlin. After the Soviet troops have left, German forces assigned to NATO can be stationed in the former GDR but without "nuclear weapon carriers." This does not apply to dual-capable conventional weapon carriers that have been equipped and designated solely for conventional purposes. Furthermore, foreign armed forces, nuclear weapons, and their carriers will not be stationed or deployed in this part of Germany once the Soviet withdrawl has been completed. (Owing to last minute wranglings over the precise meaning of this latter limitation, particularly whether it permitted exercises by non-German forces, a separate minute was appended to the treaty which states that any questions arising from the application to the term "deployed" will be decided in a reasonable and responsible way by the government of the united Germany.)

Article 6. This underscores Germany's sovereign right to membership in alliances of its choice.

Article 7. This article formally terminates the four powers' rights and responsibilities relating to "Berlin and Germany as a whole." All related quadripartite agreements, decisions, and practices are likewise ended, along with the dissolution of related institutions. Accordingly the united Germany will have full sovereignty over its internal and external affairs. (This article, however, makes no mention of allied rights stemming from existing tripartite and bilateral agreements.)

Articles 8, 9, 10. The treaty will be subjected to ratification or acceptance by all signatories and will enter into force once all the contracting parties have completed this process. The treaty will apply to the united Germany, which will act as its depository.

The full text of the treaty and agreed minute follows.

Treaty on the Final Settlement with Respect to Germany, Signed in Moscow on September 12, 1990

The Federal Republic of Germany, the German Democratic Republic, the French Republic, the Union of Soviet Socialist Republics, the United Kingdom of Great Britain and Northern Ireland and the United States of America,

Conscious of the fact that their peoples have been living together in peace since 1945;

Mindful of the recent historic changes in Europe which make it possible to overcome the division of the continent;

Having regard to the rights and responsibilities of the Four Powers relating to Berlin and to Germany as a whole, and the corresponding wartime and post-war agreements and decisions of the Four Powers;

Resolved in accordance with their obligations under the Charter of the United Nations to develop friendly relations among nations based on respect for the principle of equal rights and self-determination of peoples, and to take other appropriate measures to strengthen universal peace;

Recalling the principles of the Final Act of the Conference on Security and Cooperation in Europe, signed in Helsinki;

Recognizing that those principles have laid firm foundations for the establishment of a just and lasting peaceful order in Europe;

Determined to take account of everyone's security interests;

Convinced of the need finally to overcome antagonism and to develop cooperation in Europe;

Confirming their readiness to reinforce security, in particular by adopting effective arms control, disarmament and confidence-building measures; their willingness not to regard each other as adversaries but to work for a relationship of trust and cooperation; and accordingly their readiness to consider positively setting up appropriate institutional arrangements within the framework of the Conference on Security and Cooperation in Europe;

Welcoming the fact that the German people, freely exercising their right of self-determination, have expressed their will to bring about the unity of Germany as a state so that they will be able to serve the peace of the world as an equal and sovereign partner in a united Europe;

Convinced that the unification of Germany as a state with definitive borders is a significant contribution to peace and stability in Europe;

Intending to conclude the final settlement with respect to Germany;

Recognizing that thereby, and with the unification of Germany as a democratic and peaceful state, the rights and responsibilities of the Four Powers relating to Berlin and to Germany as a whole lose their function;

Represented by their Ministers for Foreign Affairs who, in accordance with the Ottawa Declaration of 13 February 1990, met in Bonn on 5 May 1990, in Berlin on 22 June 1990, in Paris on 17 July 1990 with the participation of the Minister for Foreign Affairs of the Republic of Poland, and in Moscow on 12 September 1990;

Have agreed as follows:

ARTICLE 1

(1) The united Germany shall comprise the territory of the Federal Republic of Germany, the German Democratic Republic and the whole of Berlin. Its external borders shall be the borders of the Federal Republic of Germany and the German Democratic Republic and shall be definitive from the date on which the present Treaty comes into force. The confirmation of the definitive nature of the borders of the united Germany is an essential element of the peaceful order in Europe.

(2) The united Germany and the Republic of Poland shall confirm the existing border between them in a treaty that is binding under international law.

(3) The united Germany has no territorial claims whatsoever against other states and shall not assert any in the future.

(4) The Governments of the Federal Republic of Germany and the German Democratic Republic shall ensure that the constitution of the united Germany does not contain any provision incompatible with these principles. This applies accordingly to the provisions laid down in the preamble, the second sentence of Article 23, and Article 146 of the Basic Law for the Federal Republic of Germany.

(5) The Governments of the French Republic, the Union of Soviet Socialist Republics, the United Kingdom of Great Britain and Northern Ireland and the United States of America take formal note of the corresponding commitments

and declarations by the Governments of the Federal Republic of Germany and the German Democratic Republic and declare that their implementation will confirm the definitive nature of the united Germany's borders.

ARTICLE 2

The Governments of the Federal Republic of Germany and the German Democratic Republic reaffirm their declarations that only peace will emanate from German soil. According to the constitution of the united Germany, acts tending to and undertaken with the intent to disturb the peaceful relations between nations, especially to prepare for aggressive war, are unconstitutional and a punishable offence. The Governments of the Federal Republic of Germany and the German Democratic Republic declare that the united Germany will never employ any of its weapons except in accordance with its constitution and the Charter of the United Nations.

ARTICLE 3

(1) The Governments of the Federal Republic of Germany and the German Democratic Republic reaffirm their renunciation of the manufacture and possession of and control over nuclear, biological and chemical weapons. They declare that the united Germany, too, will abide by these commitments. In particular, rights and obligations arising from the Treaty on the Non-Proliferation of Nuclear Weapons of 1 July 1968 will continue to apply to the united Germany.

(2) The Government of the Federal Republic of Germany, acting in full agreement with the Government of the German Democratic Republic, made the following statement on 30 August 1990 in Vienna at the Negotiations on Conventional Armed Forces in Europe:

The Government of the Federal Republic of Germany undertakes to reduce the personnel strength of the armed forces of the united Germany to 370,000 (ground, air and naval forces) within three to four years. This reduction will commence on the entry into force of the first CFE agreement. Within the scope of this overall ceiling no more than 345,000 will belong to the ground and air forces which, pursuant to the agreed mandate, alone are the subject of the Negotiations on Conventional Armed Forces in Europe. The Federal Government regards its commitment to reduce ground and air forces as a significant German contribution to the reduction of conventional armed forces in Europe. It assumes that in follow-on negotiations the other participants in the negotiations, too, will render their contribution to enhancing security and stability in Europe, including measures to limit personnel strengths.

The Government of the German Democratic Republic has expressly associated itself with this statement.

(3) The Governments of the French Republic, the Union of Soviet Socialist Republics, the United Kingdom of Great Britain and Northern Ireland and the United States of America take note of these statements by the Governments of the Federal Republic of Germany and the German Democratic Republic.

ARTICLE 4

(1) The Governments of the Federal Republic of Germany, the German Democratic Republic and the Union of Soviet Socialist Republics state that the united Germany and the Union of Soviet Socialist Republics will settle by treaty the conditions for and the duration of the presence of Soviet armed forces on the territory of the present German Democratic Republic and of Berlin, as well as the conduct of the withdrawal of these armed forces which will be completed by the end of 1994, in connection with the implementation of the undertaking of the Federal Republic of Germany and the German Democratic Republic referred to in paragraph 2 of Article 3 of the present Treaty.

(2) The Governments of the French Republic, the United Kingdom of Great Britain and Northern Ireland and the United States of America take note of this statement.

ARTICLE 5

(1) Until the completion of the withdrawal of the Soviet armed forces from the territory of the present German Democratic Republic and of Berlin in accordance with Article 4 of the present Treaty, only German territorial defence units which are not integrated into the alliance structures to which German armed forces in the rest of German territory are assigned will be stationed in that territory as armed forces of the united Germany. During that period and subject to the provisions of paragraph 2 of this Article, armed forces of other states will not be stationed in that territory or carry out any other military activity there.

(2) For the duration of the presence of Soviet armed forces in the territory of the present German Democratic Republic and of Berlin, armed forces of the French Republic, the United Kingdom of Great Britain and Northern Ireland and the United States of America will, upon German request, remain stationed in

Berlin by agreement to this effect between the Government of the united Germany and the Governments of the states concerned. The number of troops and the amount of equipment of all non-German armed forces stationed in Berlin will not be greater than at the time of signature of the present Treaty. New categories of weapons will not be introduced there by non-German armed forces. The Government of the united Germany will conclude with the Governments of those states which have armed forces stationed in Berlin treaties with conditions which are fair taking account of the relations existing with the states concerned.

(3) Following the completion of the withdrawal of the Soviet armed forces from the territory of the present German Democratic Republic and of Berlin, units of German armed forces assigned to military alliance structures in the same way as those in the rest of German territory may also be stationed in that part of Germany, but without nuclear weapon carriers. This does not apply to conventional weapon systems which may have other capabilities in addition to conventional ones but which in that part of Germany are equipped for a conventional role and designated only for such. Foreign armed forces and nuclear weapons or their carriers will not be stationed in that part of Germany or deployed there.

ARTICLE 6

The right of the united Germany to belong to alliances, with all the rights and responsibilities arising therefrom, shall not be affected by the present Treaty.

ARTICLE 7

(1) The French Republic, the Union of Soviet Socialist Republics, the United Kingdom of Great Britain and Northern Ireland and the United States of America hereby terminate their rights and responsibilities relating to Berlin and to Germany as a whole. As a result, the corresponding, related quadripartite agreements, decisions and practices are terminated and all related Four Power institutions are dissolved.

(2) The united Germany shall have accordingly full sovereignty over its internal and external affairs.

ARTICLE 8

(1) The present Treaty is subject to ratification or acceptance as soon as possible. On the German side it will be ratified by the united Germany. The Treaty will therefore apply to the united Germany.

(2) The instruments of ratification or acceptance shall be deposited with the Government of the united Germany. That Government shall inform the Governments of the other Contracting Parties of the deposit of each instrument of ratification or acceptance.

ARTICLE 9

The present Treaty shall enter into force for the united Germany, the French Republic, the Union of Soviet Socialist Republics, the United Kingdom of Great Britain and Northern Ireland and the United States of America on the date of deposit of the last instrument of ratification or acceptance by these states.

ARTICLE 10

The original of the present Treaty, of which the English, French, German and Russian texts are equally authentic, shall be deposited with the Government of the Federal Republic of Germany, which shall transmit certified true copies to the Governments of the other Contracting Parties.

AGREED MINUTE TO THE TREATY ON THE FINAL SETTLEMENT WITH RESPECT TO GERMANY OF 12 SEPTEMBER 1990

Any questions with respect to the application of the word "deployed" as used in the last sentence of paragraph 3 of Article 5 will be decided by the Government of the united Germany in a reasonable and responsible way taking into account the security interests of each Contracting Party as set forth in the preamble.